HIDDEN HISTORY
of
VINCENNES & KNOX COUNTY

HIDDEN HISTORY
of
VINCENNES & KNOX COUNTY

Brian Spangle

Published by The History Press
Charleston, SC
www.historypress.com

Copyright © 2020 by Brian Spangle
All rights reserved

Front cover: Interior view of one of the Roughan grocery stores. Glenn Roughan founded the chain in Vincennes in 1912. *Norbert Brown Collection.*
Back cover: The old Main Street Bridge over the Wabash River was constructed in 1867–68 and dismantled in 1932. *Knox County Public Library's McGrady-Brockman House*; Colorful painting of the restored Old State Bank building by artist Eve Jurgens. *Knox County Public Library's McGrady-Brockman House.*

Permission to republish the columns herein granted by the *Vincennes Sun-Commercial*.

First published 2020

Manufactured in the United States

ISBN 9781467145558

Library of Congress Control Number: 2019951873

Notice: The information in this book is true and complete to the best of our knowledge. It is offered without guarantee on the part of the author or The History Press. The author and The History Press disclaim all liability in connection with the use of this book.

All rights reserved. No part of this book may be reproduced or transmitted in any form whatsoever without prior written permission from the publisher except in the case of brief quotations embodied in critical articles and reviews.

Contents

Acknowledgements	9
Introduction	11

I. 1890s–1910

1. Bierhaus Home a Remnant of a Different Time	15
2. Dr. Charles Sanford's Story Became a Part of Local History	19
3. Dr. Von Knappe and the "Castle" on the Corner	22
4. Buffalo Bill's Wild West Came to Town in 1898	25
5. Pearl Buttons Were Once Manufactured in Vincennes	29
6. Legacy of "Uncle Joe" Roseman Can Be Seen in Knox County Cemeteries	32
7. Vincennes Native "Hub" Smith Was Diplomat and Composer	35
8. Pritchett Case Was One of the Most Unusual in County History	38
9. Vincennes Patrolman Killed after Touching Live Wire	41
10. Location of Fort Sackville Was First Marked in 1905	44
11. Vincennes Came to the Aid of Earthquake-Devastated San Francisco	47
12. Bloodhounds Helped Fight Crime in Knox County and Beyond	50
13. Destructive Hailstorm Caused Damage in Northern Knox County	52
14. A 1909 Streetcar Accident Resulted in Fatality	54

II. 1910–1920

15. The Abernathy Boys Came to Town in 1910 — 59
16. Stibbins's Murder Shocked Knox County Residents in 1911, Part 1 — 62
17. Stibbins Brothers Stood Trial for Murder, Part 2 — 65
18. Verdict Reached in Stibbins's Case, Part 3 — 68
19. Glenn Roughan Had One of Vincennes's Twentieth-Century Success Stories — 70
20. Murder at the Savoy Made Headlines in 1912 — 73
21. Theatrical Men's Friendship Was Commemorated for Years — 75
22. Bridge Watchman LaCoste Had a Challenging Job — 79
23. Vincennes Cemeteries Named in Contest — 82
24. Bowers-Lescher Sanitarium Once Served Medical Needs of Knox County People — 84
25. Christmas 1914 Saw First Vincennes Municipal Christmas Tree — 87
26. History-Making Race at the Fairgrounds — 89
27. Production of *Alice of Old Vincennes* Was Part of 1916 Centennial Celebration — 91
28. First Vincennes Public School Razed — 94
29. Vincennes Police Department Acquires First Motorized Vehicle — 97
30. Arnold's Hobby Brought Happiness to Thousands — 99
31. Ruth Jordan Served as Nurse Overseas during First World War — 102
32. Men Fail in Attempt to Rob Bruceville State Bank — 106
33. Bruno the Bear Made His Home in Vincennes for Many Years — 108
34. "Cornstalk Killing" Frightened the Community in 1919, Part 1 — 110
35. Local Man Confessed to Infamous Murder, Part 2 — 113

III. 1920–1930

36. Story from the 1920s Became One of the Most Bizarre in Local History — 117
37. Franklin Roosevelt Spoke to Voters at the Knox County Courthouse — 120
38. Checkers Champ Banks Competed in Vincennes — 123
39. Old Post Laundry Was an Innovation for Vincennes — 125

40. St. Louis Cardinals Played the Bicknell Braves 127
41. Fox Drives Were Once an Important Part of Rural Life 129
42. President Warren Harding Passed through Knox County 131
43. Edwardsport Bank Cashier Murdered in Attempted Robbery,
    Part 1 134
44. Accused Murderers Brought to Justice, Part 2 137
45. "Gentleman Jim" Made a Brief Stop at Union Depot 139
46. Local Students Took Part in Spelling Bees 141

IV. 1930–1940
47. Cooking Schools Were Once Held in Vincennes 145
48. Miniature Golf Was a Popular Pastime Locally
    Beginning in 1930 147
49. Nancy Gardner Baker Was Last Vincennes Civil War Nurse 149
50. Daniel Hanes Was Symbol of a Bygone Era 151
51. Knox County Girl Named Champion in
    International Canning Contest 153
52. Vincennes Mayoral Election of 1934 Was a Nail-Biter 155
53. Sally Rand Brought Her Risqué Show to the
    Pantheon Theater in 1935 157
54. The 1936 Heat Wave Was the Worst in History, Part 1 160
55. All-Time Record High Temperature Reached Locally, Part 2 162
56. Turtle Derby Was an Amusing Civic Undertaking 164
57. Vincennes Took in Evansville Flood Refugees in 1937 166
58. William Strange Was One of the Last Knox County
    Civil War Veterans 169
59. Duke Ellington Took the Stage at Vincennes 171

V. 1940–1950
60. Main and Busseron Streets Became One-Way 177
61. Knox County Townships Plagued by Mosquitoes 180
62. Vincennes High School Graduates of 1882 Recognized 183
63. Abbott and Costello War Bond Day 186
64. Vincennes CCC Camp Lasted Just a Few Months 188
65. Castor Beans Were Grown in Knox County
    During the Second World War 190
66. Coogan Stationed at George Field in 1944–45 192
67. Father Flanagan Brought His Message to Vincennes 195

VI. 1950–1960s

68. Vincennes City Hall Razed	201
69. Local Landmark Came Crashing Down in 1952	204
70. Vincennes Welcomed "Citizen" Truman	207
71. The 1955 Peach Crop Killed by Frigid Early Spring Weather	209
72. "Uncle Billy" Green Jr. Was Grandma Moses of Vincennes	211
73. Davy Crockett Craze Hit Locally	214
74. Old State Bank Building Was Once Truly Hidden History	217
Selected Bibliography	219
About the Author	221

ACKNOWLEDGEMENTS

Virtually all of the research for this book was done at the Knox County Public Library's regional history/genealogy research center, the McGrady-Brockman House. Opened to the public in 2002, this facility has combined collections from numerous other local libraries and is now the place to go for research in Vincennes. The collections contained there are truly massive, consisting of books, including a room full of family histories; city directories; original Knox County records, dating from the 1790s; architectural drawings; scrapbooks; pamphlets; postcards; photographs; and, most importantly for this researcher, Vincennes newspapers on microfilm from 1806 to the present.

It is often said that newspapers are the first draft of history, and it would not have been possible to write the columns that make up this book without them. It is not only the availability of the papers but also the variety of stories told and the detail that reporters early in the twentieth century added. Much of what is included in this book would have been lost had one or more newspapers not been covering all the happenings in Knox County and if dedicated people not seen to their preservation, through microfilming and now digitization. Until the 1940s, there was more than one paper publishing concurrently in Vincennes, so this gives the added benefit of getting more than one version of the same story.

The library's collection of city directories also proved invaluable in tracing individuals, their addresses and occupations over the decades.

Acknowledgements

The majority of the images that appear in the book are also from the Knox County Public Library's McGrady-Brockman House collection. Thanks to Norbert Brown for the loan of some photos I needed as my deadline approached, most notably the cover image.

Having retired from the library in 2016, I was fortunate in that I was already familiar with the resources there. Knox County is fortunate to have this wonderful research library.

Thanks go to the *Sun-Commercial* for permission to reprint these columns, all of which, with one exception, originally appeared in that publication. One piece is original to this book.

Lastly, thanks to *Sun-Commercial* readers, who often tell me that they read and enjoy the column each week.

Introduction

It is hard for me to believe that February 2019 marked twenty years since I began writing my weekly "Our Times" column on Vincennes and Knox County history for the *Vincennes Sun-Commercial*. Over those two decades, the column has undergone many changes, from overall length, to its location in the paper, to the day it is published. One thing that has stayed the same is the column's scope, which is twentieth-century history (although I haven't been able to resist going back into the 1890s for some stories that were just too good to pass up). The column was originally the brainchild of then *Sun-Commercial* managing editor Bernie Schmitt, who, back in 1999, liked the idea of examining a century of history then coming to a close.

Today, "Our Times" continues to be published, now on Saturdays under managing editor and publisher Gayle Robbins, and after one thousand–plus columns and counting, there are still many stories to tell.

Readers of the column know that I mostly write about the first half of the century, and that is reflected in this book, with only a few columns here covering events that took place after 1950.

The focus of the book is hidden history and includes a selection of columns that might not typically make the standard history books. These include columns on once prominent local people whose names have been lost to history, well-known entertainers and politicians readers will be surprised to learn once visited Vincennes, murder cases that have been long forgotten, early iconic buildings that have since been razed and columns that can best be described as "offbeat." Some of my favorite pieces have always been the latter, among them the story of Bruno, a black bear who made his home in Vincennes in the 1920s.

While my writing is more heavily focused on the city of Vincennes, there are many pieces that describe happenings throughout Knox County, such as the time the St. Louis Cardinals came to Bicknell to play the Bicknell Braves and the murder of Edwardsport Bank cashier Charles Wright in 1923. These and many others are included here.

The most challenging part of putting this book together was finding photographs to accompany some of the columns. When the topic is hidden history, it isn't likely that there will be many images of the events recounted. It has always surprised me, for instance, that, considering how many famous people passed through Vincennes in the first decades of the twentieth century, there are virtually no photographs of them in the city. Certainly, people must have taken pictures—perhaps they didn't survive or are still tucked away out there in someone's attic. In some instances, I have relied on images from the Library of Congress, specifically in the cases of Buffalo Bill, Franklin Roosevelt, Sally Rand and others, that were not taken locally, just to give readers an image that they can associate with that particular column. In some instances, I have also used contemporary photographs.

Overall, the purpose of the book is both to educate and entertain, and it is certain that readers will come away having learned some things about Vincennes and Knox County that they previously didn't know.

PART I
1890s–1910

I
Bierhaus Home a Remnant of a Different Time

Today, the Charles Bierhaus home at Sixth and Seminary Streets, although suffering years of neglect, remains one of Vincennes's iconic buildings. Constructed in 1893–94, it is an imposing edifice even today. When the home was completed, newspapers of the day were almost lacking in superlatives to describe it.

Bierhaus, a partner with his brother, John, in their father's wholesale grocery business Edward Bierhaus & Sons, certainly had the means to erect such a grand home, although there is no record of exactly how much he spent.

He chose that location for the house, it being the most fashionable part of Vincennes in those days. Many fine homes were built in that neighborhood at the turn of the century. Each had immaculate lawns that stretched down to what were then unpaved streets. There are even early postcard views touting the beauty of that part of the city. The imposing home of Joseph L. Bayard (now Klein Real Estate) stood just across from the Bierhaus lot.

Bierhaus selected a prominent out-of-state architect, Samuel Hannaford, of Cincinnati, to design the brick house in the Queen Anne/Colonial Revival style. Hannaford was architect for many important buildings in Cincinnati, as well as more throughout the Midwest, New England and the South. His work included a number of courthouses, among them Indiana's Vigo County Courthouse

John Hartigan and Peter Sertel, both local contractors, received the construction contract. It was Sertel's last job, as he became seriously ill during construction. He died in 1899.

Postcard view of North Sixth Street at the turn of the century. This was the "fashionable" part of Vincennes. *Knox County Public Library's McGrady-Brockman House.*

Ground was broken for the Bierhaus home in the summer of 1893, and the family moved in just over a year later. Charles and his wife, Helen, had two daughters, Ida and Helen. They had at least one live-in domestic worker, which was common for wealthy families at that time.

The *Vincennes Commercial* called the house "A Palace" and "A Queen Among Dwellings," further describing it as "grandly beautiful" and "stately and magnificent."

From the reception hall, the grand staircase, the pocket doors, carved woodwork, marble bathrooms, leaded glass windows and chandeliers, every feature of the house inspired awe. It was illuminated by both gas and electricity, and there were speaker tubes and call buttons to communicate between rooms.

One of the most talked about parts of the home was a large conservatory on the first floor filled with plants and flowers that imbued the entire house with their scent.

Many elegant events were held there. Helen Bierhaus was a prominent member of the Vincennes Fortnightly Club, and the Fortnightly often held functions there prior to the purchase of its own clubhouse on Buntin Street in 1915. Construction of the present clubhouse at Sixth and Seminary Streets took place in 1928.

The palatial Bierhaus home as it appeared circa 1909. *Art Work of Central Indiana.*

The Bierhaus home in 1983, after it had been turned into an apartment house. *Knox County Public Library's McGrady-Brockman House.*

It was an honor for the Bierhaus family when, in 1909, a photo of the house appeared in the book *Art Work of Central Indiana*, which features prominent homes and natural wonders in the state.

Charles Bierhaus died at the home in 1911, at the age of fifty-six, but his widow lived on there until the mid-1920s before moving to California, where she died in 1941. The house then stood vacant for several years. In the mid-1930s, it was converted into an apartment house by Clyde Richardson, and it remained apartments, with different owners and under different names, for most of its history. It was known variously as Tower Apartments, Madson Apartments and Michael Jordan Apartments. In the 1980s, a small restaurant called the Peach Tree Palace, along with a gift shop, also operated there.

Although today the old Charles Bierhaus home is a sad relic of an earlier time, fortunately, the house did not meet the fate of some of the other opulent homes that once lined North Sixth Street. Charles's brother, William, had an equally impressive house next door just across Seminary Street. It was torn down in 1966. That once grand home, with a ballroom on the third floor, had also been turned into apartments prior to being razed.

Lumber yard owner M.A. Bosworth had an ornate Victorian home on the southwest corner of Sixth and Hart Streets that was also torn down. At one time, three homes stood on Sixth Street between Seminary and Hart Streets. Piankeshaw Place Apartments now takes up the entire portion of that block. Ground was broken for Piankeshaw in 1971.

2

DR. CHARLES SANFORD'S STORY BECAME A PART OF LOCAL HISTORY

If one drives into Vincennes's Greenlawn Cemetery and turns on the first road to the left, one will see the small monument of Dr. Charles A. Sanford in the shade of a sycamore tree. The monument is inscribed with Sanford's birth and death dates. Sanford was born on January 1, 1868, and died at the age of twenty-nine on November 19, 1896. As Sanford was a member of the local Masonic lodge, the monument also features the traditional Masonic emblem of compass and square.

Dr. Sanford's bittersweet story was first told in the June 1, 1941 edition of the *Vincennes Sun-Commercial*. In May 1950, Allie Arnold, who himself became part of the narrative, recounted it on his *Old Timer* radio program that was broadcast over WAOV. The text of Arnold's broadcast was published in the local newspaper the *Valley Advance* on October 24, 1978.

Here is the story of how the young doctor came to rest in Greenlawn Cemetery, with some added detail from sources that weren't readily available in Arnold's day.

It was May 1896, when Dr. Charles A. Sanford, a native of New York, and his new bride moved to Vincennes from Falls Village, Connecticut. Dr. Sanford established a medical practice, taking the place of Dr. Lyman Beckes, who went to New York and later Germany to do postgraduate work. His office was at Fifth and Main Streets, and he lived in a home across the street, where the Pantheon Theater was later constructed. Sanford's practice grew, and he became popular in the community.

Dr. Charles Sanford's monument in Vincennes's Greenlawn Cemetery. *Author's collection.*

That autumn, an epidemic of diphtheria hit the area. Dr. Sanford worked hard to care for the many residents, especially children who were ill, finally contracting the disease himself. Other local doctors tended him, and his wife maintained a vigil at his bedside, but after suffering from the illness for two weeks, Sanford died on the morning of November 19.

In an obituary that appeared in the *Vincennes Commercial*, the doctor was described as "a sober, intelligent Christian man." The *Daily Sun* called him "a quiet unassuming young man."

At that time, the law did not allow a body to be transported across state lines if the cause of death had been a communicable disease; thus, Sanford was interred in Greenlawn Cemetery after his funeral the next day. The following local doctors served as pallbearers: Charles W. Benham, Joseph L. Reeve, James McDowell, Joseph Somes, Schuyler C. Beard, William H. Davenport and Joseph W. Smadel. All were from Vincennes, except Dr. Reeve, who lived at Edwardsport.

Not long after her husband's death, Mrs. Sanford went back east and, it was said, never returned to Vincennes.

This is where the story takes an interesting turn. After Sanford's death, his friend and community leader Guy McJimsey anonymously placed flowers on the grave each Memorial Day (then popularly known as Decoration Day) to honor the doctor and the work he had done for the community. McJimsey faithfully undertook this task for the next two decades.

In December 1917, McJimsey confided his secret to Allie Arnold, who was then a newspaperman working for the *Vincennes Capital*, asking him to take over the Memorial Day tradition. Arnold did so, also performing it in secret. Typically, in those days, peonies were the flower of choice for decorating graves.

McJimsey, who had initiated the custom, moved to California in 1930 and died there in 1936.

Arnold eventually revealed the story of the special tribute to some members of Vincennes Masonic Lodge No. 1, and for many years, the Masons continued placing flowers on the grave. Thus, for decades, a young doctor's dedication, which cost him his life, was remembered and memorialized by Vincennes people.

3
Dr. Von Knappe and the "Castle" on the Corner

The imposing Romanesque Revival house on the northwest corner of Sixth and Perry Streets, known to many Vincennes residents as "the castle" because of its resemblance to such an edifice, was built in 1904 and was originally the home and office of Dr. Wilhelm Von Knappe.

Dr. Von Knappe and his wife, the former Olivia Thrall, came to Vincennes from St. Augustine, Florida, in 1897. Von Knappe first set up his practice as a homeopathic physician in an office at Fifth and Main Streets and also resided there.

A native of Columbus, Ohio, the doctor had an impressive résumé and obtained his medical education from colleges in Columbus, Chicago and New York. He continued his training in several hospitals in Europe.

A turn-of-the-century photograph of Von Knappe shows a somewhat unconventional appearance, with the doctor sporting a bushy, unruly moustache that droops midway down his lapels.

Dr. Von Knappe initially advertised: "Diseases of the Nose, Throat, Lungs and Stomach a Specialty." In later years, his treatments expanded to "Diseases of the Eye, Gall Stones, Appendicitis, Cancer, Piles, Goitre, Rheumatism, Neuralgia and Syphilis."

In 1898, Von Knappe purchased the lot on the corner of Sixth and Perry Streets (400 North Sixth Street), where he built his stately home of Bedford limestone with stained-glass windows. He kept his Main Street office for several years after the house was constructed, eventually moving it to his residence. Patients used the Perry Street entrance.

Contemporary view of Dr. Von Knappe's "castle" at Sixth and Perry Streets. *Author's collection.*

Dr. Von Knappe had one extreme eccentricity, and in September 1917, it got him into embarrassing legal trouble. Although he often displayed his patriotism by flying a large American flag from the top of his house, it seems that, for some unknown reason, the doctor had an irrational hatred of Abraham Lincoln, even to the extent that he refused to carry Lincoln pennies. While everyone knew about this illogical behavior, it was a pamphlet Von Knappe published that slandered the assassinated president that was his undoing.

Portrait of the eccentric Dr. Wilhelm Von Knappe. *Vincennes in Picture and Story.*

There remained a true veneration of Lincoln during these years. This, coupled with the patriotic fervor that accompanied the United States' participation in the First World War, converged to anger people in the community when the pamphlet's existence became known. Von Knappe was indicted on a charge of "Libeling the memory of Abraham Lincoln, deceased." On September 13, he was arrested, brought before the circuit court judge, entered a plea of not guilty and was released on a $250 bond. On April 27, 1918, just prior to the start of his trial, Von Knappe changed his plea to guilty of "printing and distributing obscene literature." He was fined $25.00 and court costs—a total of $34.50—and the sensational case came to an end.

The couple didn't have any children. In fact, Dr. Von Knappe was known to dislike children as much as he disliked Lincoln. Youth in his neighborhood, while likely fearful of the peculiar physician, still tormented him at Halloween.

Dr. Von Knappe resumed his practice following the arrest but was said to be broken in health and spirit. He died at his Sixth Street home at the age of seventy-seven on January 13, 1924. As was typical in that day, the funeral was held at the residence. Burial was in Fairview Cemetery.

Olivia Von Knappe lived on at the house until the mid-1930s, later residing at 1142 Buntin Street. She died at Good Samaritan Hospital at the age of eighty-three on August 18, 1948.

In 1939, Rex and Flossie Thorne converted the Von Knappe home into a facility for health baths. They offered Swedish baths and hydrotherapy treatments. This business operated for only a short time.

Local people perhaps best remember the imposing building as the home and office of Dr. Norman E. Denny. Denny, also an osteopathic physician, lived and practiced medicine there for over a half century. The house has mostly been a private residence in recent years. For a brief time in the early 2000s, a used bookstore called Turn the Page operated there.

4
BUFFALO BILL'S WILD WEST CAME TO TOWN IN 1898

It was the fall of 1898, and local people were excited about a special visitor who was coming to Vincennes. On Friday, October 7, William F. "Buffalo Bill" Cody, arguably the most recognizable figure in the world at the turn of the century, brought his Wild West Show to town.

William Cody was the true embodiment of the American frontier. Born in Iowa in 1846, Cody was a Pony Express rider, an army scout, a prospector and a buffalo hunter (earning him his nickname) before trying his hand at entertainment. Buffalo Bill first traveled as part of a theatrical show and appeared on stage in Vincennes in both 1881 and 1882.

It was Buffalo Bill's Wild West Show, formed in 1883, that brought Cody worldwide fame. A true extravaganza that included hundreds of people, horses and a herd of buffalo, it appeared all across the United States and Europe, bringing a glimpse of the Old West to millions of people. Britain's Queen Victoria saw the show in 1887.

Even the logistics of moving the show from town to town was a massive undertaking. The huge production was all carried on two trains. By the late 1890s, it comprised some five hundred people, along with the livestock. They even traveled with their own grandstand seating.

There were two shows that day, at 2:00 and 8:00 p.m., each lasting two hours, preceded by a morning street parade. Even though a light drizzle was falling, city streets were packed for the parade, what the *Vincennes Commercial* called a "jam of humanity." Buffalo Bill himself headed the procession, nodding to acknowledge the cheers of the spectators.

The shows were staged in an open field on Fairground Avenue (what is now Washington Avenue), next to the recently completed Orphan's Home at the corner of Fairground Avenue and St. Clair Street (where the KCARC Civitan Children's Center is now located). The price was fifty cents for adults and twenty-five cents for children. Reserved seats were one dollar.

What the *Commercial* described as "the biggest crowd which was ever massed in this city" turned out, coming from all over the area. The city swelled with the crowds. The numbers were genuinely astounding, with an estimated 16,000 people at the afternoon show and 8,000 there that night. The population of Vincennes was only 10,249 in 1900.

William "Buffalo Bill" Cody, circa 1911. Cody drew enormous crowds when he brought his Wild West Show to Vincennes in 1898. *Library of Congress, Prints and Photographs Division, Washington, D.C.*

The show began with an overture by the famous Buffalo Bill Cowboy Band under longtime bandleader William Sweeney (one-time resident of Vincennes).

There were features that had become standard parts of the show, such as an Indian attack on a covered wagon and subsequent rescue of the settlers, a reenactment of Custer's Last Stand, frontier girl equestrian riders and a herd of buffalo being hunted by Indians. Cowboys did demonstrations, such as roping and riding bucking broncos.

A big component of the show was the Congress of Rough Riders of the World, which had been added in 1892. This consisted of mounted soldiers from all over the world. Besides members of the Sixth U.S. Cavalry and the Fifth U.S. Artillery, this included Mexican vaqueros, Argentine gauchos, Arabian acrobats and horsemen, German cuirassiers, Royal Irish Lancers, Russian Cossacks and a Cuban color guard.

One of the major draws at Buffalo Bill's Wild West Show was sharpshooter Annie Oakley, whose fame nearly exceeded that of Cody. The five-foot-tall Oakley's shooting skills were unrivaled. This is what the *Vincennes Sun* said about her exhibition at the show: "Miss Annie Oakley illustrated such dexterity in the use of firearms, as caused the expert gunner to open his eyes in wonder. She rarely missed the flying clay bird."

William "Buffalo Bill" Cody demonstrating his shooting ability on horseback in 1907.
Library of Congress, Prints and Photographs Division, Washington, D.C.

A second sharpshooter, Johnny Baker, who was with the show throughout its history, also performed, and Cody showed his own skill with a gun, shooting glass balls while riding horseback.

Immediately after the second show, the entire production was packed up and moved on to the next venue.

By the early twentieth century, the appeal of Cody's Wild West Show began to fade, in part due to the coming of motion pictures. The show went into bankruptcy in 1913. The famous showman died in Denver on January 10, 1917, at the age of seventy and was interred on Lookout Mountain, Colorado.

5

PEARL BUTTONS WERE ONCE MANUFACTURED IN VINCENNES

In the early twentieth century, mussel fishers were flocking to the Wabash River and adjacent streams in search of freshwater pearls, which could bring big prices from eastern buyers. There was also money to be made from selling the mussel shells to manufacturers who made mother-of-pearl buttons.

It was in the final years of the nineteenth century that the manufacture of pearl buttons began in the United States. Buttons had previously been imported from Europe. In fact, in 1890, no pearl buttons were made in this country, but by 1902, over fifty pearl button factories were in operation, the majority of them in Iowa. The city of Muscatine, Iowa, on the Mississippi River became the center of the pearl button industry. Muscatine was known as the Pearl Button Capital of the World. Mussel shells from Vincennes were shipped there.

In 1903, Vincennes businessmen established a button factory at First and Willow Streets. Construction of the factory (what was really just an unpretentious frame building) started in April 1903, and it was soon up and running. At that time, mussel shells were selling for from ten to twelve dollars a ton. During the first few months, the factory was only cutting buttons. It didn't yet have the capability to turn out a finished product.

In November of that same year, the business was reorganized and incorporated as the Wabash Pearl and Specialty Company (known by locals simply as the "button factory") with a capital stock of $9,000 divided into 180 shares of $50 each. There were thirteen shareholders

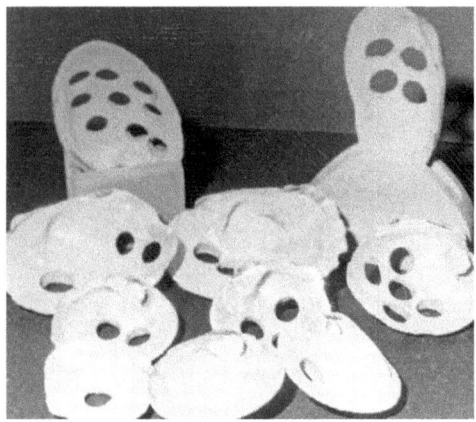

Above: Mussel shells being loaded for transport to the Iowa button factories. *Knox County Public Library's McGrady-Brockman House.*

Left: Mussel shells after the pearl buttons have been cut. *Knox County Public Library's McGrady-Brockman House.*

and seven directors. The directors were Joseph L. Ebner, Anton Simon, Francis Schenker, Simon Kixmiller, Eugene Aubry, Claude C. Winkler and Lawrence J. Weisenberger.

After incorporation, the factory began turning out finished buttons. Shells first went to the cutting room, where water-cooled circular saws were used to cut the buttons. In the finishing room, the buttons were divided up by size, ground to a particular thickness and placed in a machine that put in grooves and punched holes. They were then put through a polisher and glazer. By 1905, the factory was equipped with twenty cutting lathes and three finishing machines. About twenty people were employed there, including women, who sewed the finished buttons onto cards.

By early 1905, the factory could produce 1,800 gross of finished buttons a week. Most of the people employed there did piecework; thus, their pay was based on how much they produced.

In July 1906, due to losses, the Wabash Pearl and Specialty Company went out of business, but that summer, another small button works was being built by John and Joseph Ueding at the corner of Third and Bayou Streets. That button factory operated successfully for many years.

The cost of the shells, of course, fluctuated, but in the spring of 1918, the price had increased to thirty-two dollars a ton.

The Third Street factory eventually closed, but in 1926, Fabius Gwin of Shoals, who owned several button factories, established a new factory on the site. Gwin was a prominent Martin County attorney and served in the state legislature.

The old factory building was torn down, and ground was broken for a new building in late May. It was completed that summer, and the basement was filled with shells ready to be cut. The Gwin Pearl Button Company was run by Gwin's son Fabius Jr.

The Gwin factory closed on July 1, 1930, but reopened in 1933, providing much-needed jobs during the Depression. Those doing piecework there could expect to make about fifteen dollars a week. It also gave a steady source of income to Wabash mussel fishers.

The Gwin button factory continued to operate until the mid-1940s. Fabius Gwin died at the age of eighty on August 20, 1947, following an extended illness. For many decades, the building housed Vincennes Electric Motor Service and, in more recent years, the Fraternal Order of Police Lodge.

6
Legacy of "Uncle Joe" Roseman Can Be Seen in Knox County Cemeteries

Joseph Roseman, known affectionately as "Uncle Joe," was perhaps the best-known Knox County veteran of the Civil War. Roseman not only played a major role in postwar veterans' activities, but he also devoted much of his time to perpetuating the memory of local veterans by seeing that their graves were marked with government headstones. Anyone who visits a cemetery in Knox County will likely see a military marker ordered from the government by Uncle Joe.

Born in Knox County on June 22, 1839, Roseman started his military service when the war began in 1861, as a member of Company G, Fourteenth Indiana Infantry. He was a musician and played the fife. The Fourteenth saw action in many of the war's major campaigns.

It was in 1879 that Congress began furnishing markers for veterans in nonfederal cemeteries, the standard white marble stones that we are all familiar with (although the style would change slightly over the years). Roseman submitted the requisition forms for the stones and became the local agent authorized to receive them and see that they were properly placed. There are items in local newspapers throughout the first two and a half decades of the twentieth century noting large and small shipments of government markers coming in on the train for Uncle Joe.

In January 1903, he took charge of an enormous shipment from Rutland, Vermont, composed of 116 markers weighing a total of 30,900 pounds. The stones were placed throughout the county. Besides the city cemeteries and Catholic cemetery in Vincennes, they went to Bruceville, West Salem and Thorne Cemeteries, the Upper Indiana Presbyterian Church Cemetery and the Indiana Presbyterian Church Cemetery.

Left: Civil War veteran Joseph Roseman seen in his later years as a member of the Grand Army of the Republic. *Knox County Public Library's McGrady-Brockman House.*

Right: Joseph Roseman also received a military marker following his 1932 death. Roseman is buried in Vincennes's Greenlawn Cemetery. *Author's collection.*

In October 1908, eight markers arrived from Lee, Massachusetts. These were also distributed among several cemeteries in both Knox County and Lawrence County, Illinois.

Although Roseman was especially dedicated to marking the graves of the rapidly dwindling numbers of local Civil War veterans, most of whom he knew personally, he worked to acquire stones for all Knox County veterans and some outside the county, as far back as the Revolutionary War.

In 1921, Roseman was successful in obtaining a government marker for William Lindsay Sr., who had fought in the American Revolution. Upon his death in 1836, Lindsay was interred in the city cemetery (now Greenlawn Cemetery) with an ordinary limestone marker. Roseman offered this sentimental quote when the new stone arrived: "The winds will gradually kiss the name of William Lindsay away, but the government's honor stone of white marble will for ages show where William Lindsay, who fought with general George Washington for liberty, lies sleeping." Ironically, today a visit to Greenlawn shows that the government stone is less readable than the original grave marker.

Roseman could never have imagined that over a half century following Robert E. Lee's surrender at Appomattox, he would be ordering stones for men who lost their lives on the battlefields of France in the First World War, a war that saw the use of tanks, airplanes, mustard gas and other previously inconceivable weaponry. Many markers also went to men who succumbed to influenza in the army camps.

In August 1918, Roseman took delivery of eight stones: six for Civil War veterans, as well as stones for then servicemen Lawrence Bouchie and Ellis Cannon, who both died of pneumonia that past February. Bouchie was laid to rest in Mount Calvary Cemetery and Cannon in Fairview Cemetery.

By late 1922, Roseman had obtained more than 1,300 military markers for local veterans.

It was said that he kept a book that included the names of deceased veterans from the Revolution through the First World War, who rested in Vincennes cemeteries.

Uncle Joe Roseman died at his Broadway Street home at the age of ninety-two on March 31, 1932. He was interred in Greenlawn Cemetery and, naturally, has a military stone marking his grave. One of his two sons, Andy, a veteran of the Spanish-American War who died in 1937, is buried near him, also with a military marker.

7
VINCENNES NATIVE "HUB" SMITH WAS DIPLOMAT AND COMPOSER

In the pre-dawn darkness of March 6, 1903, a Baltimore and Ohio Southwestern train pulled into Union Depot carrying a sealed casket holding the remains of Vincennes native Hubbard Taylor Smith. Smith had achieved distinction in two varied careers, working overseas for the U.S. Department of State and composing music. He had most recently served as vice and deputy consul-general in Cairo, Egypt.

In the fall of 1902, Smith was taken ill with kidney disease. By mid-January 1903, his condition had deteriorated to the point where he had to be transported by steamer to Nice, France, for treatment. Smith never made it to the French city, but rather had to be taken off the ship at Genoa, Italy. He died in a hospital at Genoa on February 9 at the age of forty-eight.

Hubbard Taylor Smith (called "Hub" by those who knew him well) was born in Vincennes on March 29, 1854. He attended Vincennes University, although he did not graduate. He eventually pursued government work and, on January 10, 1876, was appointed general-service clerk in the War Department. The story told is that he got the job solely on the strength of the elegant handwriting he used on his application. He held many positions (too many to recount here) in the Census Office (now Census Bureau), Treasury Department and Department of State.

Some of the highlights of his career were his roles as deputy consul-general at Paris and at Constantinople; vice-consul at Osaka and Hyōgo, Japan; vice-consul at Canton (Guangzhou), China; and, lastly, vice and deputy consul-general at Cairo.

Left: Portrait of Vincennes native Hubbard Taylor Smith. Smith had an illustrious career as a diplomat prior to his untimely death in 1903. *Knox County Public Library's McGrady-Brockman House.*

Right: Jewel presented to Hubbard Taylor Smith by the Chinese following his service in that country as American vice-consul. *Knox County Public Library's McGrady-Brockman House.*

Smith also gained fame through his talents as a composer. He composed around two hundred songs and instrumental pieces. Among his best-known songs were "Listen to My Tale of Woe," "Swinging in the Grapevine Swing" and "Sweethearts and Wives." The latter song became popular in the naval service and was sung on New Year's Day.

Local newspapers carried accounts of Smith's medical condition in the days leading up to his death. On February 10, his father received word of his son's passing through several telegrams sent from Washington, D.C. One of the telegrams came from Secretary of State John Hay.

The body was shipped by steamer from Genoa on February 19 and arrived in New York on March 4, where it was met by Hub's brother Cyrus and a friend from the War Department, who traveled with it to Vincennes. The casket was immediately taken to the family home at 523 Main Street.

Smith was survived by his father, Dr. Hubbard Madison Smith; two unmarried sisters, Alice and Mary; and brothers Curtis, of Dallas, Texas; and Cyrus, of Indianapolis.

The funeral took place at the First Presbyterian Church on March 7, a dreary, rainy day. Some of Smith's own songs were sung at the service. Of course, given the circumstances, the casket remained closed.

One of the most noteworthy aspects of the funeral was the number of flowers, some of the largest and most elaborate arrangements ever seen locally. Some of the displays were collected at Washington, D.C., when the train passed through that city.

Smith was buried in the family lot in the city cemetery (now Greenlawn Cemetery). The next day, hundreds of people paid their respects at the grave.

8
PRITCHETT CASE WAS ONE OF THE MOST UNUSUAL IN COUNTY HISTORY

For many years, the family of James and Ella Pritchett resided in a two-story house at 811 Broadway Street in Vincennes. James was a prominent local attorney. It was no surprise that the couple opposed construction of the new Knox County Jail that opened in 1903 adjacent to their property at Eighth and Broadway Streets. Only a couple of years after the jail was built, Ella Pritchett, through her husband, sued the county for damages over alleged disturbances that the jail's prisoners were causing.

It was in July 1905 that the suit was filed against the Board of Knox County Commissioners, Sheriff Abraham Westfall and jailor Edward Busching. Mrs. Pritchett claimed that the prisoners would look through the jail's large windows into their home and call out to the family and their guests, using what was described as "profane and indecent language." Some even threw things out the windows.

Further, the clanking of the iron doors of the jail was considered an annoyance.

Mrs. Pritchett was asking for $7,000 in damages. Not surprisingly, the case left Knox County on a change of venue to Gibson County and was later moved to Sullivan County. The judgement was made on November 10, 1906, in favor of the defendants.

Pritchett took the case all the way to the Indiana Supreme Court, where he eventually won an injunction preventing the sheriff from opening any of the eighteen windows that faced their property on the jail's east side. This was quite a hardship for the jail's prisoners and employees, especially during

1890s–1910

Present-day view of the old Knox County Jail at Eighth and Broadway Streets, now the probation department. *Author's collection.*

hot weather in those pre–air conditioning days. Further, a tall fence was to be constructed between the two buildings.

The injunction remained in effect for the next thirty years, as Ella Pritchett continued to occupy the house. (James Pritchett passed away in 1914.) When Ella died in 1937, at the age of eighty-five, her children, Wright Pritchett and Edna Julian, inherited the house. At that time, the Knox County Commissioners considered purchasing the property as a home for the county welfare department, but there was opposition to the deal and funding was not approved by the county council.

Meanwhile, in January 1938, the Pritchett heirs sued the county in superior court claiming that the decades-old injunction was being violated. They were seeking $5,000 in damages. The suit brought against the Board of County Commissioners, Sheriff Clarence "Gus" Joice and jailor David Phillips was moved to Gibson County. There would be no action taken in the case, as the property had been sold at a tax sale in 1936. In February 1938, it was purchased by Sheriff Joice after the Pritchetts failed to redeem it—although Joice let the family continue residing there for a time.

The Pritchett house at 811 Broadway Street in Vincennes was razed in 1981. The house caused many legal woes for Knox County officials. *Knox County Public Library's McGrady-Brockman House.*

At the start of 1941, the commissioners again attempted to get funding to buy the Pritchett house. In May, the county council finally approved the $2,600 purchase. Not only did the county get additional office space, but the injunction that had gone into effect all those years ago came to an end as well.

The house was then remodeled at a cost of $3,000. That price included a new roof and furnace. The Knox County Welfare Department moved in in late December of that year.

The Welfare Department remained in the former Pritchett house for many years. The building later stood vacant for a time and was finally razed in 1981 when the new county jail was constructed.

9
VINCENNES PATROLMAN KILLED AFTER TOUCHING LIVE WIRE

An electrical storm hit Vincennes on the night of Sunday, August 6, 1905, bringing with it wind and rain and creating all kinds of problems with the city's lights and phone system. Ironically, it was two days later that electrical damage resulting from the storm led to the death of a local police officer.

It was late on the evening of August 8 that Vincennes patrolman Harrison "Harry" B. Wells was walking his beat, beat No. 4, which took in the area around the Union Depot Hotel. Wells, at the age of forty, was one of the senior men on the force. He was also a big man, standing five feet, eleven inches tall and weighing 250 pounds. Just before midnight, Wells saw that an arc lamp was out at Twelfth and Harrison Streets.

For many years, in most communities, carbon arc lamps were used for lighting streets and other big spaces, such as factories. They not only put out a bright light but also were economical compared to other types of lighting.

In those days, it was the responsibility of city patrolmen to report if a streetlight was not burning. Sometimes an officer could simply shake the wire, repositioning the carbon and illuminating the lamp, which is what Wells attempted to do. Unfortunately, the wires had become crossed in the storm, and the line that Wells grasped was live.

Edna Lloyd and Frank Cady were on Miss Lloyd's porch nearby and saw what happened. They heard Wells cry out and saw him fall in the gutter. Frank Foncannon lived across the street, and his phone was used to call for help. Local physician Dr. Clarke Stewart arrived on the scene,

Vincennes Patrolman Harrison "Harry" Wells, who died after touching a live wire in 1905. Pictured with him is his wife, Mary, and daughter Verna (*middle*). *Courtesy of the Vincennes Police Department.*

but Wells, who had gasped a few times, was already dead. The only visible sign of trauma was his severely burned left hand. A second patrolman later accidentally touched the wire and was knocked down by the force of the jolt, but he was uninjured.

Lloyd and Cady were the only witnesses to Wells's death. Both said that Wells had jerked the wire, causing the lamp to light. It then went out, and he jerked it again, which is when he was electrocuted.

By that time, despite the late hour, a crowd had gathered on the street corner. County Coroner David Buley arrived, and the body was taken to Dexter Gardner & Son mortuary.

Wells was survived by his wife, Mary, and a sixteen-year-old daughter, Verna Irene.

The funeral was held at the family home at Tenth and Oak Streets on August 10. Reverend William G. Law of the First Baptist Church had charge of the service. Wells was originally from the northern part of Knox County.

(He was born in Sullivan County in 1865.) His remains were transported by train to the Edwardsport town cemetery for burial. The following police officers served as pallbearers: Harry Adams, Henry Nieters, Asa Evans, George W. Cralle, William Swayze, Fred Wise and Ulysses Steenberger. Both Swayze and Nieters had come to offer help the night of the tragedy.

Wells reportedly had two good life insurance policies. One paid his widow $1,000 and the second $1,500, considerable sums of money in 1905.

That autumn, Wells's daughter, Verna, just two weeks after turning seventeen, married Herman Miller, a Knox County farmer. Mary Wells never remarried. She died at the age of sixty-seven at her daughter's rural Vincennes home on May 13, 1933, and was buried alongside her husband at Edwardsport.

10

LOCATION OF FORT SACKVILLE WAS FIRST MARKED IN 1905

On the afternoon of Saturday, November 18, 1905, a group of interested citizens gathered on the west side of First Street in Vincennes, between Church and Barnett Streets, for a special ceremony. It was on that day that the Daughters of the American Revolution (DAR) dedicated a monument to mark the site of old Fort Sackville. The British fort was captured by George Rogers Clark and his men in 1779, opening up the Northwest Territory for American settlement. Over 125 years after that historic event, Clark's accomplishment was being memorialized in stone.

In those years, the area where the fort had once stood was covered with decrepit buildings, with nothing to denote its significance in history. That all changed in 1905, when the DAR set about marking the site. Local members who worked to acquire the marker were: Mrs. Reuben G. (Sarah) Moore, Miss Mary Love, Mrs. Samuel B. (Emma) Judah and Mrs. William F. (Mary) Calverley.

The stone, the carving and the land on which it was placed were all donated. The marker, of Indiana limestone, measuring six feet high, three feet wide and two feet thick, was donated by the Bedford stone quarries. Peter J. Burns, of the Standard Monument Works in Vincennes, carved the inscription and set the stone at no cost. Local businessmen John and Charles Bierhaus allowed it to be placed on their property.

The ladies of the DAR paid for the bronze plaque attached to the top of the stone, which read, "Site of Fort Sackville." The inscription carved by Burns had the following words: "Captured by Col. George Rogers

1890s–1910

Left: Marker placed on South First Street in 1905, commemorating the site of Fort Sackville. The log cabin in the background was later used by the Boy Scouts. *Knox County Public Library's McGrady-Brockman House.*

Below: The old Fort Sackville marker as it looks today next to the George Rogers Clark Memorial. *Author's collection.*

Clark from the British Feb. 25, 1779. Resulting in the U. S. Acquiring the Great Northwest Territory Embracing the States of Indiana, Ohio, Illinois, Michigan, Wisconsin, and Minnesota."

The dedication ceremony began with a parade that formed at city hall at Fourth and Main Streets. In the line of march was the First Regiment Band; Vincennes University Cadets; members of the Grand Army of the Republic; and automobiles and carriages carrying DAR members, program participants, city officials and guests. Three of the city's oldest residents, Dr. Hubbard Madison Smith, Dr. Reuben G. Moore and Elbridge G. Gardner, rode in one carriage.

The weather was fine for the unveiling, and a sizeable crowd turned out. Speakers for the event were local attorney C.B. Kessinger (in place of Mayor George Greene, who could not attend) and Tarquinia L. Voss, of Indianapolis, state DAR regent. Short elevated platforms had been placed on each side of the marker, and Robert Moore, grandson of Sarah Moore, and Emily Jane Judah, granddaughter of Emma Judah, stood on each side and removed the American flag covering the stone. The Vincennes High School quartet then sang "America," with accompaniment by the First Regiment Band. Next, Sarah Moore spoke briefly, formally presenting the monument to the city.

One special guest for the unveiling was Eunice Bedell, of Mount Carmel, Illinois. Bedell was a "true" daughter of the Revolution, as her father had seen service in the war.

Fast-forward a quarter century, and in 1929, the area where the marker stood was being cleared for construction of the massive George Rogers Clark Memorial. The old limestone marker was removed and left on a pile of rubble, where it stayed for a number of years. Prior to the dedication of the memorial in 1936, the Clark Memorial Commission asked local contractor Austin P. Snyder to retrieve the stone and reset it on the memorial grounds. That work was done on May 14, with the memorial dedicated exactly one month later. The stone base, which had read "Erected by the Daughters of the Revolution, Nov. 18, 1905," was lost. The marker was set just to the right of the memorial steps, where it can still be seen today.

II

VINCENNES CAME TO THE AID OF EARTHQUAKE-DEVASTATED SAN FRANCISCO

Early on the morning of April 18, 1906, the city of San Francisco, California, then with a population of around 400,000, was devastated by one of the worst earthquakes in history. The quake, which measured 8.3 on the Richter scale, caused a massive fire that destroyed much of the city.

The statistics recorded in the aftermath of the earthquake are truly astonishing. For years, the official death toll was given as between 700 and 800 people, but later estimates have placed the number in excess of 3,000. It was estimated that 28,000 buildings were destroyed, and 225,000 people, over half the city's residents, were left homeless. The total loss in property damage exceeded $400 million (and that was 1906 dollars).

Communities all across the country, appalled by the devastation and suffering, donated money to aid San Francisco, with gifts totaling millions of dollars.

Vincennes mayor George Greene took an informal poll of prominent taxpayers in order to determine if they would approve of the city making a monetary gift to assist San Francisco. The mayor received an overwhelmingly positive response and sent a letter to the Board of Public Works requesting $500 for that purpose.

The mayor's letter read, in part, "Let it not be said of Vincennes as a municipality, and of us as citizens and officials, that we were the last of the many thriving cities in Indiana to heed these cries. Let us contribute our mite, as it were, toward alleviating the sufferings and allaying the anguish of the people of the far distant Pacific slope. And let us do so without further delay."

Damage to homes from the 1906 San Francisco earthquake. *Library of Congress, Prints and Photographs Division, Washington, D.C.*

On April 21, the board, then composed of Edward Watson, George Borrowman and John B. Zuber, voted to give that sum, the motion made by Zuber. Two days later, at its April 23 meeting, the Vincennes City Council agreed unanimously to appropriate the money.

At Sunday services, on April 22, three local Catholic churches took up a collection for victims. At St. John's German Catholic Church, eighty dollars were collected, and the Old Cathedral took in sixty-five. At St. Thomas, thirty-seven dollars were given.

Besides assisting the populace of San Francisco, there were immediate concerns about local people who were in California at the time. As the *Vincennes Commercial* wrote in its April 19 edition: "There are many Vincennes people living or visiting in San Francisco and other cities and towns in the California earthquake zone, and tidings from them are awaited by anxious relatives and friends here."

It took time, of course, for mail to get across the country, and telegraph service was delayed because of the quake. Telegrams finally began reaching Vincennes from California over Western Union on April 23. On that day, Mary Spaulding had word from her son, Joseph, who had been in San Francisco at the time of the quake, that he was uninjured. Edward Smith also had a telegram on the twenty-third from his son-in-law Lieutenant Lee Purcell, informing him that he and his wife were fine. Purcell was stationed at the Mare Island Naval Shipyard northeast of San Francisco. Others also had word that relatives were safe.

Letters eventually began arriving too, such as the message on a postcard received by Dora Thompson, the sister of James Reel, on April 26. Reel was from Knox County but lived in San Francisco. He informed his sister that his family had lost everything in the earthquake.

Plans were quickly made for rebuilding San Francisco, and a more modern city rose in its place.

12

BLOODHOUNDS HELPED FIGHT CRIME IN KNOX COUNTY AND BEYOND

The early weeks of the year 1907 saw much criminal activity taking place in Knox County. In February, both the Sandborn and Oaktown Post Offices had their safes blown, and at the end of March, the Knox County Treasurer's Office was robbed. In those days, due to their unsurpassed sense of smell, bloodhounds were the principal means of tracking suspected criminals.

Since the county didn't have its own bloodhounds, dogs often had to be brought in from other areas. After these three crimes were discovered, bloodhounds from the town of Lynnville, down in Warrick County, were sent for and brought in on the train to do the tracking.

Although the need for local bloodhounds was great, they were a significant investment. That April, four men—Knox County sheriff Abraham Westfall, court bailiff Dave Byers, riding bailiff Oscar Thompson and police commissioner George Gardner—combined their resources and purchased a pair of dogs from a breeder in San Antonio, Texas. The cost was $250 (equivalent to nearly $7,000 in today's money). The dogs were used for tracking in Knox County and rented out to communities outside the county, helping the owners recoup some of their costs. Even before the pair arrived, the Town of Pleasantville put in a call for their use in a big arson investigation.

The dogs, which had previously been employed on a convict train, were delivered on April 30 and taken to the jail, then located at Eighth and Broadway Streets, where they were to be housed. Both dogs were under two years old. The male was named Red, because of his coloring, and the female's name was Lizzie. They had the typical long, floppy bloodhound ears, which drew much comment. The dogs were a source of pride for the community, with one newspaper boasting that they were "more competent looking" than the Lynnville hounds.

The bloodhounds were immediately given some exercise and described as showing "a great deal of ginger." There was a call for the dogs from Russellville, Illinois, the next day, where some chicken thieves had been at work, but they weren't taken out, since their owners had not yet learned how to handle them.

The bloodhounds were finally used on May 5, when the Goodman Restaurant at Bruceville was burglarized. The dogs took the trail to the Bruceville train station ticket window, and additional detective work determined that the culprit had bought a ticket to Bicknell. The thief was later apprehended at Terre Haute. Later that same day, the dogs were again used when a Vincennes meat market was robbed of a few dollars. That time, the animals were less successful, running "a cold trail."

The four-legged crime fighters were soon being put to the test all over the area and began proving their worth. Besides being employed locally, over the course of 1907–8, communities that made use of the bloodhounds included Shoals, Loogootee and Bridgeport, Illinois, and several towns in Sullivan County. Most of the cases were burglaries of some sort. There is no record of how much the owners charged for the dogs' services.

The population of the jail increased substantially in the summer of 1908, when the female bloodhound gave birth to seven pups. The dog's owners sold the valuable pups after they were weaned, realizing a tidy profit.

Sheriff Westfall left office at the start of 1909, taking the dogs with him, although he continued to take them out on calls.

Other local people later purchased their own bloodhounds. One of these was Charles Glenn, Decker Township justice of the peace, who bought a pair of the dogs in November 1909. These animals came from Westfield, Illinois, and Glenn paid $200 for them. They were in big demand. In early 1910, they helped track a gang of chicken thieves that had been active in the county.

In later years, bloodhounds were again used locally but were brought in from outside the county. In the spring of 1935, a pair of Illinois hounds were put to work on the John F. Wampler farm, near Bicknell, after some of Wampler's hogs had been poisoned. The pair picked up a trail to a neighboring house, but no arrest was made in the case.

Even today, despite advances in technology, law enforcement across the country still rely on bloodhounds, especially in missing persons cases.

13
Destructive Hailstorm Caused Damage in Northern Knox County

Saturday, September 7, 1907, began as an ordinary late summer day in Knox County. Corn stood tall in the fields, and people from the countryside traveled to the nearest town to do their weekend trading. No one could have foreseen that a dangerous rain and hailstorm were to strike the northeastern part of the county that afternoon.

The storm, which was centered on Edwardsport, hit at about 3:00 p.m. Hail the size of hen's eggs (some stones were claimed to be baseball size) was propelled by strong winds, breaking windows, shredding cornfields and killing birds and chickens. Apples were torn from trees, gardens were ruined and there was damage to rooftops. Heavy rain washed out railroads, and trees were toppled by the wind. People hastened for cover, but many still suffered bruising from hailstones.

It was reported that one farmer was caught out in the storm while hauling wood and abandoned his wagon and team of horses. His frantic team then ran directly into the White River and drowned.

The passenger train on the Indianapolis and Vincennes Railroad was forced to stop near Edwardsport for almost a half hour due to hail covering the track. The terrified passengers huddled in the aisle, listening to the tremendous pounding on the roof and windows. Windows in the engine and some in the passenger cars were broken, raining glass on the occupants. Flying tree limbs also clattered against the windows.

The storm was about a quarter-hour in duration. Afterward, it was claimed that, in places, hail covered the ground to a depth of four inches. Hours later, ice still blanketed the ground.

The town of Freelandville was also severely affected by the hail, with gardens destroyed, and Bicknell, Westphalia and Sandborn to a much lesser extent. No precipitation at all fell in the county south of Bicknell. At Vincennes, the temperature rapidly dropped, and a chilly wind blew. People could see menacing storm clouds to the north.

Storm damage in Daviess, Dubois, Harrison, Lawrence and Orange Counties was even more severe. In Harrison County, rabbits and even hogs were killed by hail, and hogs were reportedly killed at Paoli. A horse was killed in Dubois County, and a colt died in Daviess County.

Damage to the area corn crop was in the thousands of dollars.

In the spring of 1907, a destructive hailstorm had hit the city of Vincennes, but the September 7 storm was said to be worse because the hailstones were launched by such strong winds.

14
A 1909 Streetcar Accident Resulted in Fatality

On Saturday evening, August 7, 1909, the end of a sweltering hot day at Vincennes, two friends, George Hoffman and Burt A. Curry, both traveling salesmen in town from Indianapolis, met downtown and decided to take a cooling ride on a streetcar. The first streetcar they encountered was a closed car, so they waited for an open car, what turned out to be No. 44, operated by motorman Frank Moore. It would be a fatal choice for one of the men.

Hoffman and Curry rode to Columbia Park (now Kimmell Park) but did not disembark. Rather, their intention was to go directly back to town. There were only two other passengers on board for the return trip, Joseph Finn, who worked as a cooper at the Murphy Distilling Company, and another local man, John Hicks. It was considered unusual (but, in retrospect, fortunate) for so few people to be riding from the north end at that time on a summer night. Manning the car with motorman Moore was conductor Melbourne Sharp.

Shortly after 10:00 p.m., the streetcar approached the railroad switch on North Second Street near the Central Foundry at Swartzel Avenue. There are conflicting versions of what happened next, but what is known for certain is that the streetcar pulled directly onto the track as an Evansville and Terre Haute switch train was backing some cars filled with melons down the switch in the direction of the Ebner Ice and Cold Storage Company. The train smashed into the center of the streetcar, toppling the car on its side and dragging it a short distance down the track.

There are differing accounts, as well, as to the actions of the men on board when the crash occurred—that is, whether they saw the train coming and jumped or were thrown from the car. It is uncertain if Burt Curry jumped, fell or jumped and then fell. Regardless, Curry, who was twenty-two years old, was the accident's only fatality, as the car crushed him when it turned on its side, killing him instantly.

Joseph Finn was badly injured, suffering a broken collarbone and one or more fractured ribs. The other men had less severe injuries.

People quickly gathered at the scene to give aid, as the inevitable rumors spread that many people had been killed. Gardner's Red Cross ambulance arrived and took Finn to a local hotel for treatment. Gardner's transported Curry's body to their morgue.

There were also many opinions as to where blame for the accident lay. The crossing was known to be extremely dangerous. It was called a "blind switch" and had no watchman.

A Vincennes streetcar, once an important mode of transportation in the city. In 1909, an open streetcar was in an accident that cost one man his life. *Knox County Public Library's McGrady-Brockman House.*

The streetcar men, both longtime employees, said that they did not see the train until they were on the track. Moore then tried to get across, but it was too late.

There was a report that the train's brakeman had motioned for the car to stop, but the warning was ignored. It was also noted that the conductor had failed to exit the car to see if the track was clear.

The August 1909 accident was one of the worst to ever occur on the Vincennes streetcar line and the first to result in the death of a passenger. Curry's body was returned to family in Indianapolis.

Knox County coroner Norman E. Beckes conducted an inquest into Curry's death, taking testimony from several witnesses. Beckes filed his verdict on August 13, finding fault with both the railroad and the streetcar company. His verdict read, in part: "I find that neither the Vincennes Traction and Light company nor the E. & T.H. Railroad company exercised the necessary precautions to prevent an accident."

As might be expected, a rash of drawn-out lawsuits followed. Perhaps the most significant was that brought by Burt Curry's father, William, against the Vincennes Traction Company. William Curry sued for $10,000 in damages. That case went on a change of venue to Daviess County, where both plaintiff and defendant waived a jury trial. The case was decided by Daviess County Circuit Court judge J.W. Ogdon, who on May 20, 1912, awarded Curry a judgment of $1,500.

PART II

1910–1920

15
THE ABERNATHY BOYS CAME TO TOWN IN 1910

On the afternoon of Sunday, May 1, 1910, brothers Louis "Bud" and Temple "Temp" Abernathy, ages ten and six, respectively, rode into Vincennes on their cow ponies. The boys had started their trip in Oklahoma and were heading to New York to see former president Theodore Roosevelt on his return from his African safari and European tour. Their father, John, was a United States marshal in Oklahoma and a friend of Roosevelt's. Roosevelt had appointed him to the position while president.

The boys started their trip on April 5, and it had taken them nearly a month to reach Vincennes. They typically made forty to fifty miles each day but had traveled only thirty miles the day of their Vincennes stop. From St. Louis to Cincinnati, they were mostly keeping to the route of the Baltimore and Ohio Railroad. They bought a map every time they crossed into a new state.

After stabling their horses, the pair walked to the Grand Hotel at Third and Busseron Streets, where they spent the night. Temple was not tall enough to reach the hotel register, so the desk clerk had to sign his name for him.

The *Vincennes Sun* described the boys this way: "The diminutive fellows dressed in wide brimmed hats and leather boots coming up to their knees attracted considerable attention. Both are small for their ages, but make up for this fact in their ability to take care of themselves. They are not afraid of anything."

In fact, outside the Grand, a local boy hit Temple, and the latter immediately had his fists up to fight, until hotel guests stopped the altercation.

Statue of the Abernathy boys in Frederick, Oklahoma. *Frederick, Oklahoma Chamber of Commerce.*

Both their appearance and their unique story drew people to them, all of whom had questions. They were said to be polite to everyone they encountered, always answering with "yes sir," or "no sir."

Louis wrote to his father every day, and they often wired him for money to pay their bills.

That night, they were treated to a film about Roosevelt that was playing at the Colonial Theater at Fourth and Busseron Streets, although Temple could see the screen only by standing on a chair.

They always got an early start, getting up at 6:00 a.m. On the morning of the second, they departed Vincennes and made their way through Washington, headed for North Vernon.

The boys made it to New York in time to see Roosevelt, who arrived there on June 18. While in that city, they bought a car, a Brush Runabout, had their horses shipped home on the train and actually drove back to Oklahoma. The return trip took them twenty-three days.

This was not the first trip the pair had taken alone, nor would it be their last. In 1909, they traveled on horseback from Tillman County, Oklahoma, to Santa Fe. In 1911, they took up the challenge of riding horseback from the Atlantic to the Pacific in at least sixty days, with a prize of $10,000 at stake. Although the trip took them sixty-two days and they failed to win the prize, they still established a record. Finally, in 1913, they rode an Indian motorcycle from Oklahoma to New York City.

Both of the Abernathys lived long, full lives. Bud became a lawyer and Temple an oilman. Bud died on March 6, 1979, and Temple on December 10, 1986.

The exploits of the Abernathy boys made them famous in their day, with newspapers in communities along their route writing about the brothers. Even though books about them have been published, including *Bud & Me: The True Adventures of the Abernathy Boys*, by Alta Abernathy, Temple's wife, today, their names are mostly unknown outside of Oklahoma. A statue of the boys can be seen in the town of Frederick, Oklahoma.

Stibbins's Murder Shocked Knox County Residents in 1911, Part 1

On the evening of Friday, November 17, 1911, the body of sixty-four-year-old George Stibbins, a prominent Harrison Township farmer, was found sprawled in the mud of his barn lot, where he had gone to feed his livestock. Stibbins was dead from a bullet to the back of the head. His body was by the corncrib door, where he had been putting corn in a bucket when the shot was fired. Hogs rooted around his remains, and a lantern he had held lay at his side.

The body was discovered by two of his children, Ray, age twenty-three, and Georgia, just fourteen, who had gone to look for their father when he was so long in returning to the house. The Stibbins farm was located several miles south of Monroe City in the area known as Calmuck. George Stibbins and his wife, the former Nancy "Nannie" Bartlow, had married in 1878. There was another son, Slater Edward (called Edward), who was thirty years old, and three more daughters: Nellie, Lucy and Anna. A third son, Ernest, died at the age of twenty-two in 1909.

Suspicion immediately fell on family members. Following the murder, there were many unusual actions on their part. The children returned to the house after the awful discovery, and Edward was sent for help, during which time their father's body lay where it fell. No attempt was made to pursue a possible assailant, and the sheriff wasn't even notified until Saturday. In fact, it had been up to authorities to inform the widow that her husband had been shot. Further, all of the family members denied even hearing the shot.

A revolver was later found lying in the mud at the scene.

All kinds of theories regarding the family's behavior that night were floated. Many suspected that the reason the body was left in the barn lot so long was so that it would be mutilated by the hogs, thus destroying evidence.

The killing made public the dissension, already well known by neighbors, that had been rife within the family. There had been major disagreements, most notably over how the farm should be run. In fact, the sons had previously tried to have their father declared insane so they could take over the farm.

An investigation into the crime was undertaken by Knox County deputy sheriff William Ohnemus, prosecuting attorney Shuler McCormick and Vincennes superintendent of police Thomas Robertson.

On November 19, Edward was arrested for the crime, although the evidence against him was considered circumstantial. The next day, he was arraigned in the justice of the peace court on a charge of murder in the first degree, entering a plea of not guilty. Edward was a college graduate and had worked as a teacher, including for a time at Edwardsport. It was known that he and his father had had a rocky relationship, and George had banned his son from sleeping in the house (although he would often sneak in and stay the night).

Edward was confined in the Knox County Jail and not allowed to attend his father's funeral, which was held from the home on November 21. Burial was in Hamline Chapel Cemetery. Some family members visited Edward at the jail the next day, and he employed noted Indianapolis attorney Eph Inman to defend him.

Monument of the murdered George Stibbins in Hamline Chapel Cemetery overlooking the Harrison Township countryside. *Author's collection.*

The next twist in the case occurred two days later, on the morning of November 24, the day after Thanksgiving, when Ray Stibbins was visiting his brother at the jail and he too was arrested on the same charge. Ray Stibbins had not attended college but had always worked on the farm. He married Nealy Stafford in 1907 and lived in a home just a short distance from the Stibbins farm. Edward had been living with the couple at the time of the murder. In fact, one key piece of evidence was footprints coming from their house to the barn and back.

George Stibbins's will, which he made on October 11, 1910, was probated on December 11. He left everything to his wife. Upon her death, his estate was to be divided equally among his six children.

In the final weeks of 1911, legal proceedings began, all leading up to the brothers' sensational murder trial in April of the following year.

17
STIBBINS BROTHERS STOOD TRIAL FOR MURDER, PART 2

On November 17, 1911, wealthy Harrison Township farmer George Stibbins was found shot to death in his barn lot. His sons Edward and Ray were later arrested for the crime and confined in the Knox County Jail.

Legal proceedings against the brothers began on December 12, with a preliminary hearing held before a packed house in the council chamber at city hall before presiding judge Levi F. Purky, a justice of the peace. A long list of witnesses was called, including Stibbins's widow, Nannie, and his daughter Georgia, who along with Ray had found the body.

The hearing resulted in the brothers being bound over to the Knox Circuit Court, without bail. A grand jury returned an indictment against them for murder in the first degree, and they were arraigned on February 15, 1912. Their attorney entered not guilty pleas for them, and their trial was set for April 9.

The trial went to Greene County on a change of venue, and on March 13, the brothers were transferred to the jail at Bloomfield.

The trial began at 9:00 a.m. that Tuesday, with the Stibbins brothers defended by four attorneys: Eph Inman, of Indianapolis; William M. Alsop, of Vincennes; Curtis Shake, then of Bicknell; and Webster V. Moffett, of Bloomfield. The prosecution was made up of Greene County prosecuting attorney James M. Hudson; William L. Slinkard, of Bloomfield; and Knox County prosecuting attorney Shuler McCormick.

Judge Charles Henderson, of the Greene and Sullivan Circuit, presided over the trial.

The Greene County Courthouse circa 1920, site of the Stibbins brothers murder trial. *The Indiana Album.*

Nearly one hundred subpoenas had been issued for witnesses, forty-nine by the state and forty-nine by the defense. Most of these were character witnesses. Family members continued to give the brothers their full support and attended the trial throughout the ordeal. The pair was described as thin and pale after having spent so many months confined in jail.

Jury selection consumed the first days of the proceedings. A twelve-man jury was finally seated on the afternoon of April 11. The men were sequestered for the duration of the trial. Most of the jurors were farmers, and they ranged in age from mid-twenties to late sixties.

The opening statement by the prosecution commenced on April 12. Witness after witness was called to give testimony—people who knew the family's history, those who came to the scene that night, law enforcement officials and later character witnesses.

The courtroom was packed each day, with standing room only. Women made up the biggest part of the audience.

The trial was big news well beyond the immediate area, and numerous reporters from other cities were in the courtroom.

Although the trial was front-page news in local papers every day, on April 14, the ocean liner RMS *Titanic* struck an iceberg and sank in the north Atlantic with the loss of more than 1,500 lives. From that time on, the proceedings were reported alongside updates of that historic event.

Most everyone agreed that the prosecution's case was largely based on circumstantial evidence. They argued, among other points, that the sons had had a strained relationship with their father. Further, their behavior the night of the murder was suspicious. They showed no grief and left the body in the hog lot. Tracks were found between the barn and Ray Stibbins's home. Overall, their key point was that the brothers killed their father to get his extensive estate.

Still, there were many more days of testimony to come and more evidence yet to be introduced in what would become the longest trial in Greene County history.

18
Verdict Reached in Stibbins's Case, Part 3

In late April 1912, following day after day of statements and testimony, the murder trial of brothers Edward and Ray Stibbins was nearing its end in the Greene County Circuit Court, where it had gone on a change of venue from Knox County. The brothers were accused of killing their father, George, on the night of November 17, 1911.

The prosecution concluded its case on April 17 by introducing evidence taken from a dictograph machine. The device had been hidden in the Stibbins boys' jail cell in Vincennes with a receiver for officials to listen in on their conversations, but even that was not revealing due to problems with the sound. It was reported that this was only the fourth trial in the United States in which dictograph evidence was introduced.

The defense began presenting its case on April 19 with an opening statement by attorney Eph Inman. Most of the Stibbins family, including the widow, daughters Nellie and Lucy, and Ray's wife, Nealy, eventually testified.

The two defendants spent hours on the stand, fervently denying their guilt. Both men broke down while giving testimony. The defense did not attempt to prove that the murder had been committed by a third party; rather, their theory was that George Stibbins had committed suicide.

One of the big mysteries in the case was the fact that authorities determined that the gun found at the scene was a .32-caliber revolver and the wound was thought to have been made by a .38-caliber gun.

Once the defense rested, lengthy closing statements began, finally concluding on Saturday, April 27. William Slinkard, one of the attorneys for the state, actually spoke, with breaks, for a total of seven and a half hours.

The excitement and interest in the case among the residents of Bloomfield cannot be overemphasized. As a reporter covering the trial for the *Vincennes Commercial* wrote in the April 28 edition, "Everybody in the town has been talking the case, from the first grade in the schools to the oldest man living here and nothing else is talked. What the town will do for entertainment when the verdict is returned is a mystery."

Factories even closed some afternoons so employees could attend the trial, and the high school let out early one Friday to allow students to hear closing arguments. Once night sessions began, a Bloomfield theater lost all business.

The consensus among Bloomfield people was that the boys would be acquitted. Some feared a hung jury.

Finally, at 10:30 p.m. that Saturday, after nineteen days, the case went to the jury, and at 5:00 a.m. the following morning, after six and a half hours of deliberations, the men reached their verdict. The verdict of not guilty was read in court by the deputy clerk at 8:10 a.m. Six ballots had been taken before the jury voted to acquit. Most everyone, the judge included, agreed that there had not been enough evidence to convict.

Upon the reading of the verdict, the courtroom erupted in pandemonium, and the Stibbins family personally came forward and thanked jury members.

After five months of turmoil, the family resumed their lives. The widow, Nannie, never remarried. She died at her rural Monroe City home on March 19, 1930, at the age of seventy-two.

On May 27, 1954, Edward was working on his farm when his clothing became tangled in a tractor and his arm was mangled. He died from his injuries six days later, and his remains were cremated. He was seventy-two years old.

Ray moved to Detroit, where he died of natural causes on November 19, 1971, at age eighty-two. His remains were returned to Knox County for burial in Hamline Chapel Cemetery.

To this day, the murder of farmer George Stibbins remains unsolved.

19

GLENN ROUGHAN HAD ONE OF VINCENNES'S TWENTIETH-CENTURY SUCCESS STORIES

Grocer Glenn Roughan had one of the big business success stories in Vincennes in the first decades of the twentieth century. Roughan established a chain of grocery stores across Vincennes and surrounding communities at a time when detractors claimed that such a business plan simply wouldn't work. Those were the days when family-owned mom-and-pop grocery stores were the norm. He proved himself way ahead of his time, completely transforming the local grocery business.

Roughan, born in 1882, was a Bridgeport, Illinois native and had owned grocery stores prior to establishing his chain. He started out working with his father, Pat, in a store in St. Francisville. Glenn Roughan later had a grocery store at Fourteenth and Main Streets in Vincennes, but he sold it and moved to St. Louis. Coming back to Vincennes, he opened a store at Twelfth and Main Streets that he eventually sold as well.

Finally, on January 1, 1912, after learning everything there was to know about the grocery business, Roughan, at the age of twenty-nine, opened what would be his anchor store at Ninth and Main Streets. That store was a success, and on July 25, 1913, a second store was opened, this one at 1602 North Second Street. A third store at 26 North Second Street was launched on April 15, 1915. On May 30, 1919, he opened a grocery store on State Street in Lawrenceville.

In 1914, a wholesale department was added to his first store.

Business was booming for Roughan Grocery Company, and growth continued unabated. At its peak, the Roughan chain comprised twelve grocery stores, eight in Vincennes, one in Lawrenceville, one in Bicknell and two in Evansville. Roughan actually became one of the biggest grocers in the state.

There were several keys to Roughan's success. First, he sold quality products at low prices, buying in bulk to supply his many stores. Second, at a time when many small grocers let customers buy on credit, he bought for cash and sold for cash. Lastly, but perhaps most importantly, was his dedication to advertising, something other grocers weren't really doing much in those years. Readers opened their Vincennes newspapers to see large Roughan ads touting his bargain prices.

An August 1916 Roughan newspaper ad listed sugar cured bacon, twenty cents a pound; a twenty-five-pound bag of granulated sugar, two dollars; a twenty-four-pound bag of flour, fifty cents; a bushel of potatoes, eighty-five cents; navy beans, eleven cents a pound; apples, twenty-five cents a peck; chicken, twenty-two cents a pound; and fresh country eggs, twenty-four cents a dozen.

In 1923, Roughan even opened a clothing store on Main Street, although that business was somewhat short-lived, closing in 1930.

The Roughan Grocery Store on the 100 block of Main Street in Vincennes as seen in June 1938. *Library of Congress, Prints and Photographs Division, Washington, D.C.*

For many summers, Roughan held a big annual picnic for employees, their families and guests at Harmony Park. In 1926, as a sign of endearment, he was presented with a silver goblet service. The presentation was made by Mayor Claude Gregg.

Following years of hard work and success, Glenn Roughan died at his home at 727 Buntin Street on October 21, 1931. He was only forty-nine years old. His cause of death was given as gastroenteritis. He was survived by his mother and a daughter, Genevieve. His wife, Perna, died in an Olney sanitarium at the age of thirty in 1919. The Roughans are buried in Fairview Cemetery.

When he died, Roughan still owned seven grocery stores: six in Vincennes and one in Lawrenceville. Clarence Piper, Glenn Roughan's brother-in-law and a longtime employee, chiefly as manager of his clothing store, was made a special administrator of Roughan's estate and given the task of temporarily running the stores. Piper and his brother, George, who also worked for Roughan, then purchased the stores, and in 1938, they formed the start of Piper Grocery Company. The Piper stores also operated in Vincennes for many years.

20

MURDER AT THE SAVOY MADE HEADLINES IN 1912

It was a murder that stunned residents of Vincennes in 1912, even though neither the murderer nor the victim made their home in the city. The *Vincennes Sun* called it a "story of unrequited love, destruction, jealousy and insanity."

On the night of September 21, 1912, one Thomas Harry Davies, thirty-six, a native of England and a professional wrestler, who had traveled to Vincennes from Chicago, killed Hazel Lucile May at the Savoy Café at 25 North Second Street. (The café stood where Old National Bank's parking lot is now located.) May was a seventeen-year-old actress who had been performing with the Knickerbocker Stock Company at the Grand Opera House. Davies had fallen in love with the young woman, but the courtship had gone sour and she spurned him. Just hours after the crime, Davies took his own life.

That Saturday, following the evening show, May and her mother, Helen, went to the café to wait on a carriage that would take them to the train depot. Their destination was Terre Haute, where the company was to appear the following day. The streets were crowded, as was typical of a Saturday. It was around 10:30 when Davies walked in, pulled a .32-caliber revolver and shot Lucile May four times. There are conflicting accounts as to whether he spoke to the victim first or just began shooting. Regardless, the young woman was dead at the scene, lying in a pool of blood on the café floor.

May was described as a "striking blond" who caught everyone's eye. She and Davies, a divorced father, had been in a relationship for two years. He first saw her on stage in Oklahoma City (which was his home). A number of letters she had written him, as well as sealed letters he had written, were among his possessions and told their story. The contents of a letter written on September 12 were the catalyst for the fatal act. In that letter, Lucile May had ended their relationship.

The crime was clearly premeditated. Davies admitted that he came to Vincennes with the intention of killing May. It was known that he was in town. In fact, he had attended both the company's matinee and evening performances.

Davies was immediately taken into custody, with an officer arresting him near Second and Main Streets. He was placed in the Knox County Jail at Eighth and Broadway Streets, where, at 1:30 a.m., he was found hanged in the jail's bull pen, having used a split towel for a noose. Suicide had been his intention all along, as witnesses at the café said that, following the murder, he had turned the gun on himself, but the weapon had jammed.

May's remains were removed to the Dexter Gardner & Son mortuary (then located at 427 Main Street), where, oddly enough, her distraught mother allowed a curious public to view the body. On Monday, the body was transported to Paris, Missouri, for burial.

Davies's remains were taken to Gardner's as well and were also shown to the public. A telegram received from Davies's brother, James, who lived in Vancouver, British Columbia, asked that the body be cremated and sent to him.

Cremation certainly wasn't common at that time, and the body had to go all the way to Cincinnati for this process. It was taken there on September 29, accompanied by George Gardner and his son Dexter and then brought back to Vincennes. This was reportedly only the fifth cremation Gardners had been involved with. The cost was twenty-five dollars.

There is one minor postscript to the story. Lucile May had a white poodle, named Midge, with her when she was killed. The dog was lost in the confusion of the night and roamed the streets for several days. She was finally found and shipped to Helen May in Missouri.

21

THEATRICAL MEN'S FRIENDSHIP WAS COMMEMORATED FOR YEARS

Minstrel shows were a popular form of entertainment in the United States from the early nineteenth century through the first part of the twentieth century. Today, such shows are seen for what they were, a part of the country's racist past. The shows, which included singers, dancers, musicians and comedy, often featured men in blackface and denigrated and mocked African Americans.

Despite their clearly racist connotations, there is a unique story to be told about a minstrel show that came through Vincennes annually. The show was the Al G. Field Minstrels, one of the most popular minstrel troupes of their day, and the story has to do with Field's friendship with local man William "Uncle Billy" Green.

William Green was one of the best-known men in Vincennes. He built Green's Opera House (later known as the Grand Opera House) at Second and Busseron Streets in 1859. The building burned in 1885 but was immediately rebuilt. It was later purchased by John T. McJimsey. When Green marked his hundredth birthday on April 17, 1912, virtually the entire town turned out to help him celebrate.

Al G. Field, born Alfred G. Hatfield in Virginia, had performed in a minstrel show before forming the A.G. Field Minstrel troupe in 1886. Field's show was an enormous success, traveling all across the country and making him a wealthy man. He and William Green became good friends, with Green always attending his Vincennes shows. Green had known Field in the days when Field was just beginning his career.

Green died on Christmas Eve 1912, just a few months after reaching his milestone birthday. The touching part of the two men's story then began. For many years following Green's death, when the Field Minstrels came to the city for a performance, as part of their street parade, they would march to his home at Seventh and Main Streets, and in his memory, the minstrel band would play "Auld Lang Syne."

Right: Al G. Field Minstrels poster circa 1900. Field's troupe appeared in Vincennes many times over the years. *Library of Congress, Prints and Photographs Division, Washington, D.C.*

Below: The William Green home at Seventh and Main Streets in Vincennes. The house was razed in 1957. *Knox County Public Library's McGrady-Brockman House.*

Opposite: William "Uncle Billy" Green with his granddaughter, Mary Tindolph. This photo was taken on December 14, 1912, ten days before Green's death at the age of one hundred. *Knox County Public Library's McGrady-Brockman House.*

Performances in Vincennes were often in late November or early December. In 1913, the troupe performed both a matinee and an evening show on Thanksgiving Day. There was a full house at both shows. The Grand seated 1,250 people.

The tradition of the minstrels playing at the Green home continued until the Grand Opera House closed in 1918, and the troupe no longer came to Vincennes, since it had no venue in which to perform. Visits resumed after the Pantheon Theater opened on Main Street in 1921.

Al G. Field died in 1921 at the age of seventy-two, and his son-in-law, Eddie Conard, then headed the troupe. Despite the fact that both Green and Field were deceased, the minstrels continued to honor the ritual of playing "Auld Lang Syne" in front of the Green dwelling.

This is how the *Vincennes Commercial* described the minstrels' December 12, 1922 visit to the old Green residence: "Despite the pinch of the cold and difficulty experienced with freezing instruments, not a word of complaint was heard which made the tribute to Mr. Green all the more reverent and touching, awakening memories of the friendship which had existed between the two theatrical men." Several of those taking part had not even known Green or Field.

The house remained in the Green family for many years following the patriarch's death. Perry and Ann Tindolph (Ann was Green's daughter) and Joseph and Molly Griggs (Molly was his granddaughter) would live in the home.

The popularity of minstrel shows eventually faded. The Al G. Field Minstrels performed at the Pantheon twice in 1927, on March 28 and again on December 16. On both occasions, they played "Auld Lang Syne" at the Green home. What was described as "a small but appreciative audience" saw the December 16 show. This seems to have been the group's last local performance.

The old Green home, where the minstrels had honored the memory of Uncle Billy Green for all those years, was torn down in 1957 to make way for the North Side Federal Savings & Loan Association building.

The Grand Opera House was razed in 1959 and is now the location of the Riverfront Pavilion.

22
Bridge Watchman LaCoste Had a Challenging Job

Mitchell LaCoste Sr. was already a well-known figure in Vincennes when he was made watchman of the Main Street Bridge in January 1914. Newly elected Republican mayor James House appointed him to the job.

LaCoste, born in 1855, was from an old French family. For a time, he and his brother, Samuel, ran a blacksmith shop at Third and Broadway Streets (where Alice Manor Apartments now stands). The ring of hammer striking anvil was a distinctive sound in that part of the city for many years. In those days, good blacksmiths had all the work they wanted. A record from 1906 shows Sam LaCoste being paid twelve dollars for shoeing the fire department's horses. Mitchell also worked for a time at the City Electric Lighting Company.

The responsibility of the bridge watchman was to oversee the bridge and handle any problems that arose. One had to be prepared for all sorts of unforeseen happenings. The Main Street Bridge, sometimes called the Wagon Bridge, was busy at all hours with both horse-drawn and automobile traffic.

There are several examples of situations LaCoste had to deal with as a watchman, from the mundane to the tragic.

In the wee hours of the morning of September 17, 1915, LaCoste had to retrieve a johnboat that he saw floating in the river and contacted the police. The boat held fishing paraphernalia, but the occupants were nowhere to be found.

Hidden History of Vincennes & Knox County

The old Main Street Bridge over the Wabash River. Early in the twentieth century, Mitchell LaCoste had the challenging job of bridge watchman. *Knox County Public Library's McGrady-Brockman House.*

On the evening of June 11, 1917, he was on duty as one of the big Lenahan gravel barges was making its way through the bridge draw, when, due to an accumulation of driftwood, it smashed into one end of the draw. LaCoste and some other men were standing on the bridge when the barge hit and feared that the whole structure would give way. The bridge held, but enough damage was done that it had to be closed until the following day.

Late on the night of October 15, 1917, LaCoste got out of bed to answer a knock on his door and found a man whose automobile had gone off an embankment and turned over a short distance from the bridge. The watchman followed his visitor to assist two other men who were still trapped in the car.

All of those incidents pale in comparison to what happened on September 25, 1916. That afternoon found the Main Street Bridge typically lined with traffic when the covered wagon of two horse traders from Illinois, heading west on the bridge, stopped when some harness broke near the Illinois approach. The two men—George Harris and his son-in-law, Frank Schumaker—who were intoxicated, became violent when they were told by another man that their wagon was blocking traffic and had to be moved. Both that man and LaCoste were struck by objects thrown by the pair. LaCoste, after being knocked down twice, then ran to his home, got his revolver and faced the men on the road in front of his house. When the two picked up bricks and began lobbing them at LaCoste, he fired, killing Harris and wounding Schumaker. Some of the men's family members were in the wagon and witnessed the entire altercation.

That night, a coroner's jury heard evidence regarding the shooting and completely exonerated LaCoste, labeling the act justifiable homicide.

LaCoste's life spanned that of the bridge. He recalled when it was built in 1867–68 and as a boy had even walked across while it was under construction. He also lived to see the old bridge come down. It was dismantled in 1932 after the Memorial Bridge opened. Mitchell LaCoste died just a few years later, on July 25, 1938, at the age of eighty-two.

23
Vincennes Cemeteries Named in Contest

Two Vincennes cemeteries, Greenlawn and Fairview, acquired their names in the early years of the twentieth century as the result of a somewhat disorganized effort on the part of city officials.

Greenlawn, long known as the old city cemetery, has burials dating from the late eighteenth century and is the resting place of notable pioneer residents, such as Francis Vigo and Elihu Stout.

Fairview Cemetery, where burials date from 1899, was for some years after its establishment simply called the new city cemetery. Thus, "old" and "new" were how the two were differentiated, although many local people wanted them to be assigned official names.

In March 1914, the Board of Cemetery Trustees responded to the public's wishes by holding a contest to let people submit prospective names for the new cemetery. At a March 5 meeting, held by the trustees, a prize of fifteen dollars was offered to the individual who entered the winning name. Mayor James House, Louis A. Meyer and George E. Gardner each gave five dollars toward the total prize. Suggested names were to be dropped off at the mayor's office by April 1. If the winning name was duplicated, then the first person to enter that name got the prize.

By the contest deadline, nearly 150 people had submitted around 500 names. On April 15, it was reported that a "secret" committee remained at work selecting a winner.

This is where the story of naming the city cemeteries takes an odd turn. Nothing was done by the board toward choosing a winning name, and as time passed, the contest was inexplicably forgotten.

1910–1920

Vincennes's old city cemetery, which was officially given the name Greenlawn Cemetery in 1919. *Knox County Public Library's McGrady-Brockman House.*

It wasn't until over five years later, in July 1919, that the contest results were unearthed and both cemeteries named by the board. The *Vincennes Capital*, in its July 22 edition, commented, "Just how the contest happened to be overlooked is not known, but the board, following numerous requests, decided to meet and decide the proposition."

The *Vincennes Commercial*, on July 23, said, "After years of slumbering over the selection of a name for the city cemetery, which was to have been decided by selection from a list furnished by contestants for $15 prize money, the cemetery trustees met and selected the name 'Fairview' for the new city cemetery and the name 'Green Lawn' for the old city cemetery."

Since so much time had passed, it could not be determined who of the eight people who submitted the name Fairview had been the first to do so, so the prize had to be divided—thus, it did not go very far.

Those who entered the name Fairview, as reported by local papers, were Charles A. Gross, Mira T. Caldwell, Gaylord S. Morse, Florence Hobble, Mrs. J.B. Wagner, Minnie Grover, Hugh Willmore and Pauline E. Hoar.

It was the board itself that designated the old city cemetery Greenlawn. Signs were installed at both cemeteries with the new names.

In 1939, a third city cemetery, Memorial Park, was opened for burials.

24
BOWERS-LESCHER SANITARIUM ONCE SERVED MEDICAL NEEDS OF KNOX COUNTY PEOPLE

In the years preceding American entry into the First World War and briefly in the postwar period, the Bowers-Lescher Sanitarium at 217 North Third Street in Vincennes was an important medical facility that treated all types of ailments and injuries. Although Good Samaritan Hospital had opened in 1908, a sanitarium was better equipped to deal with long-term patient care.

Dr. Eugene Bowers and his wife, the former Ida Oliphant, moved to Vincennes from Monroe County, Indiana, in about 1905. Dr. Bowers received his training at Barnes Medical College in St. Louis and practiced medicine in Vincennes for several years prior to opening his sanitarium. In the spring of 1913, Bowers purchased the old parsonage from the First Methodist Episcopal Church trustees to be remodeled and outfitted for the Bowers-Lescher Sanitarium. The price for the building was around $5,000.

The sanitarium began as a partnership between Bowers and Dr. Edwin Lescher. Lescher had just left his practice in Mount Carmel, Illinois. The two made a perfect fit, with Bowers performing surgeries and Lescher treating diseases and doing lab work.

The renovations, which included large additions to the building, took several months, and the new twenty-bed sanitarium finally had its opening for the public to tour on March 19, 1914.

Much expense went into creating a top-rate facility. There were Turkish and Russian baths, along with medicated baths in the basement. Patient rooms were on the first and second floors. The operating room was on the second floor, and there were sun parlors that overlooked Third Street. The

The Bowers-Lescher Sanitarium at 217 North Third Street in Vincennes circa 1916. *Views of Vincennes.*

sanitarium boasted a fifteen-kilowatt X-ray machine. The doctors had their offices on the first floor.

Several nurses staffed the sanitarium, and it even had a three-year training school for nurses. Lena Teschner was interim superintendent of nurses.

Among the many diverse conditions treated by the doctors were lockjaw, appendicitis, cancer, gallstones and broken limbs as well as burns and gunshot wounds. In December 1916, when approximately fifteen men were burned following an explosion at Bruceville's Oliphant-Johnson Coal Mine, the injured were brought to the sanitarium for care.

Dr. Lescher left the sanitarium in February 1916, selling his share of the business to Bowers. His plan was to take additional medical training and resume his practice in Mount Carmel.

In July 1916, James W. Henson, from Richmond, Virginia, came to Vincennes to partner in the sanitarium, and for a time it became known as Bowers-Henson Hospital. Henson headed the facility. Dr. Bowers discontinued doing surgery.

Interior view of the Bowers-Lescher Sanitarium's first floor circa 1916. *Views of Vincennes.*

The sanitarium closed in 1920, and for a couple of years the building was operated as a hotel, called the Homestead Hotel. In 1922, Dr. Bowers converted it into an eight-family apartment complex called Homestead Apartments. Housing was in short supply in those postwar years, so the apartments filled a real need. Dr. Bowers kept rooms on the second floor and, for a time, maintained an office on the first floor. For a brief period, he had an office in the American National Bank building on Main Street.

Bowers and his wife divorced in 1930, and in 1932 he married Receda Herman. Eugene Bowers lived on at the apartment house until his death on March 1, 1944, at the age of sixty-six. His widow and two children from his previous marriage survived him. Burial was in Memorial Park Cemetery.

Receda Bowers resided at the apartment house for many more years. She was a photographer and operated a photo studio there.

Ervin and Betty VanKirk later took over the apartment building, and from the mid-1960s to the mid-1980s, it was known as VanKirk Apartments. The structure was eventually razed and a modern apartment building constructed on the site.

25

Christmas 1914 Saw First Vincennes Municipal Christmas Tree

On Christmas Eve 1914, a huge throng of people was gathered at the corner of Fourth and Busseron Streets for the lighting of the city's big municipal, or community Christmas tree. This was the first year that Vincennes had a municipal tree, something that was increasing in popularity at that time, especially in larger cities.

A committee, with Gerald K. Smith as chairman, along with various subcommittees, was formed to oversee acquisition and placement of the tree, the accompanying program and a big relief effort for the city's less fortunate.

In 1914, there was an open lot at Fourth and Busseron Streets, to the rear of city hall, referred to as "City Hall Place." The Elks Home faced that lot. City Hall Place was chosen as the site to erect the tree.

The tree was donated by Henry Patterson, who had a farm near Fritchton. The thirty-foot-tall red cedar was selected by Vincennes street commissioner Thomas Jordan, and on December 16, two wagons were used to transport it to the city. It was put in place on the morning of December 22. A group of men using two horses and a block and tackle raised the massive cedar, which was coated in ice from sleet that had fallen.

The tree was decorated with three hundred red, white and blue incandescent lights with a big lighted star on top. Felix Cadou, superintendent of the City Electric Lighting Company, oversaw the electricians putting up the lights. The tree was actually decorated before it was put up.

On Christmas Eve, a special program was held for the lighting of the tree. One local newspaper estimated that, in spite of the biting cold, three thousand people turned out. For a half hour, from 6:30 to 7:00 p.m., all of the city's church bells rang. The ringing of the bells was followed by a fanfare of trumpets from the balcony of the Elks Home. A volunteer chorus then sang "Silent Night." Next, the tree was lit, with Mayor James House's daughter, Ruth, throwing the switch. Struck by the beauty of the lighted tree, men doffed their hats and women waved handkerchiefs.

The evening continued with more Christmas songs by the chorus and music by the Knights of Columbus Male Quartet and the First Regiment Band. The tree would remain lighted through New Year's Eve. It was sprayed at least once with water, which immediately froze, making for an even prettier scene.

In conjunction with the placement of the first municipal Christmas tree, food was collected to make the holiday merrier for the city's poor. Donations of food were stored in the City Hall Court Room, where the baskets were assembled. Coffee, flour, apples, meat, canned goods and staples, such as potatoes, were included in the baskets. Somewhere between four and five hundred baskets were delivered on Christmas Eve and Christmas morning. Churches, the Salvation Army, the Fortnightly Club and other local organizations also aided the needy.

In 2014, exactly a century after that first tree was placed, the city resurrected the idea of having a community Christmas tree downtown. The new location was the Gimbel Corner at Second and Main Streets. The tree that year was a fifty-foot-tall Norway spruce donated by Hilda Purcell. It was erected on December 6.

26
HISTORY-MAKING RACE AT THE FAIRGROUNDS

At midafternoon on Saturday, July 3, 1915, an American flag was waved signaling the start of an automobile race at the Fairgrounds (now Gregg Park) in Vincennes. The cars that crossed the starting line that day were participating in a historic event, what was said to be the first one-hundred-mile race on a half-mile track in the state of Indiana.

Three local men were promoters of the race: Vincennes mayor James M. House, Louis Wilkerson and Perry D. Green. It was advertised all over the area and attracted many out-of-town guests, filling the city's hotels. The Big Four Railroad ran two extra trains just for race fans. Some local businesses closed during the race. The *Vincennes Commercial* boasted that it would be "the greatest auto derby ever staged in Southern Indiana." That prediction turned out to be no exaggeration. On the Friday before the race, over five hundred people turned out, just to watch the drivers practice.

Seven men from Indiana and Illinois participated, each paying a five-dollar entry fee. These were: Harvey Goddart in the "Courter Special"; Jack Lanham (of Vincennes) in a Stutz; W.L. Hunt, driving a "Buick Special"; Herb Groff in a "Maxwell Special"; Bill Akin in a Buick; Al Crispen in a Buick; and Bert Ingles driving a Ford. Not all of the drivers owned their cars.

Judges were all automobile dealers: D.D. Aldrich, of D.D. Aldrich Automobiles; Marshall T. Johnson, of the Johnson Auto Company; and Marion Gould, manager of the A.L. Maxwell Company. Sol Allman, manager of the Gibson-Overland Company, was the starter, and local jeweler Justus Henkes served as official timekeeper.

The dirt track had been heavily oiled to keep the dust down. There was some rain the night before and the morning of the race, but the track emerged in good condition. Start time had been set for 1:30 p.m. but was delayed an hour or so to get the track in shape. Doctors and nurses, along with an ambulance, were on hand in case of accidents.

It was estimated that five thousand people saw the race. There were over three thousand paid admissions and many more watching from Burnett Heights. Trials immediately preceded the race itself, with positions based on the time made in one circle of the track. Harvey Goddart took the pole position. Louis Wilkerson paced the drivers one lap in his car, and the racers were off with a flying start.

Lanham and Goddart made a real race of it for a time, but Lanham went out on the thirty-fifth lap and Goddart never gave up the lead, taking the checkered flag. He finished the one hundred miles in two hours, twenty-seven minutes and fifteen seconds, averaging a then speedy forty-one miles per hour. Goddart, who was only twenty-one years old, was from Mount Carmel, Illinois, and the "Courter Special" was owned by Guy Courter, also of that city.

While the car looked like a Ford and had a Ford engine, it was actually made up of parts from many different makes of autos. It had cost $1,800 to build.

W.L. Hunt of Indianapolis came in second, just over ten minutes behind Goddart.

Al Crispen, of Sullivan, was third, about fifteen minutes behind Hunt.

Herb Groff, of Indianapolis, was fourth, the only other driver to complete the race.

While there were tires thrown and some engine trouble, as well as two cars briefly sideswiping each other, overall, the race went off with no major incidents.

The winner received $300 cash. Second place got $100, and third place $50. There were other prizes. Justus Henkes gave a pair of cufflinks to the leader at the ten-mile point, and the Gibson-Overland Company gave a pair of tires, valued at $60, to the leader after fifty miles. Duesterberg & Kramer Rexall Drug Store donated some smaller items to the leader at the seventy-five-mile point. Goddart took all of these prizes.

Overall, promoters considered the race an overwhelming success and began making plans for more races.

27

Production of *Alice of Old Vincennes* Was Part of 1916 Centennial Celebration

It wasn't just by chance that the play *Alice of Old Vincennes* was selected as the production to be staged by the senior class of Vincennes High School in 1916. That was, of course, the year marking Indiana's centennial, so the play—based on Maurice Thompson's bestseller featuring the heroine Alice Roussillon and her role in the surrender of Fort Sackville—was seen as the perfect way to launch the local celebration. The date chosen for the play, February 25, also had significance. It was on that day in 1779 that George Rogers Clark captured the fort from the British.

Lois Holt, who was actually a junior, got the lead role of Alice. Some other members of the cast were Clyde Roloff, Mildred Olin, Esther Green, Marie Mumford, Robert Moore, Lester Tolbert, Lloyd Shepard, Virgil Morris, Edward VonTress and Jules Bastin.

Much hard work went into the four-act play. Margaret Holland, a teacher at the school, and Principal John W. Foreman rehearsed with the students for several weeks. Arthur Beriault, of Indianapolis, who had appeared in the original production of the show and was a professional acting coach, assisted with the final two weeks of rehearsals, with a dress rehearsal on February 24.

Period heirlooms were borrowed from city residents to be used on the stage, including a chair that had been owned by Francis Vigo. Mary Jeanette McJimsey was in charge of stage settings.

The venue for the play was the Grand Opera House. There were two shows: an afternoon matinee that was open to local schoolchildren (many schools dismissed at noon that day), followed by an evening performance.

The cast of *Alice of Old Vincennes*, the 1916 senior class high school play. Junior Lois Holt played Alice. *1916 Vincennes High School Yearbook.*

Miss Holt especially won praise for her portrayal of Alice. The *Vincennes Commercial* wrote, "The audience was very appreciative of the fact that she acted her part with the grace and ease characteristic of a renowned actress, and presented her with several large bouquets of roses."

The play was an overwhelming success, with the Opera House completely filled for both shows. As the *Vincennes Sun* put it, the play "proved both an artistic and financial success." It was said to be much better than the professional production that came to Vincennes in 1902.

While no record seems to have survived of the cost of admission, around $425 was taken in. There were several requests for the play to be shown in other communities.

There is an interesting postscript to the story of the 1916 senior class play. Lois Holt, who played Alice, later moved from the Vincennes area but continued to entertain, even traveling with Chautauquas for a time. She was also a church choir director for many years. Lois died in Iowa at the age of ninety-five on October 18, 1995. Playing Alice all those years ago remained a highlight of her life and was even noted in her obituary published in Mason City, Iowa's *Globe Gazette*. These lines were included about the Kentucky native: "She moved to Vincennes, Ind., where she attended Vincennes High School. As a junior, she played Alice in the senior class play 'Alice of Old Vincennes' and was well remembered there for her portrayal."

Alice of Old Vincennes also became a part of the city's celebration of the state bicentennial in 2016, just as it had a century earlier, with *Alice of Old Vincennes: A Musical* premiering at the Red Skelton Performing Arts Center that Memorial Day weekend.

28
First Vincennes Public School Razed

In the final days of April 1916, the razing of a Vincennes landmark that had served the city's educational needs for over a half century began. It was that spring that workers began dismantling the old Central School that stood on Buntin Street, halfway between Sixth and Seventh Streets.

Central School, built in 1860, was the first public school in Vincennes. Bids for the school's construction were opened in March 1860. Thomas C. Turner was given the contract for the brickwork and James A. Kerr for the carpentry work. School trustees were John D. Lander, William Williamson and Gerhard H. Duesterberg.

By the beginning of June, construction was well underway, with the walls having ascended to the second story. By autumn, the building was almost complete. In its October 27, 1860 edition, the *Vincennes Gazette* reported, "The public schoolhouse is nearly enclosed, and is an ornament to the city."

The school building was three stories tall with a bell tower. Its total cost was $18,949.49. It housed all of the lower grades and later high school students. Professor H.P. Hall was superintendent, and his assistant was Anson W. Jones.

The school year, which at one time had been as short as three months, was expanded to ten months.

In 1911, in his book *History of Old Vincennes and Knox County, Indiana*, George Greene described the structure as having "withstood well the ravages of time" and said that it "presents a very good appearance to-day."

Plans had been to tear down the school after the end of the 1916 term, but in March, construction of the new George Rogers Clark School building had started, and Superintendent E.O. Maple and the school board decided

Above: The first Vincennes Public School, constructed in 1860. The building was torn down in 1916. *Knox County Public Library's McGrady-Brockman House.*

Right: Civil War veteran George Sparrow received the contract to raze the public school. *Knox County Public Library's McGrady-Brockman House.*

that since excavation of that school was so near the Central School that it was not safe for the students to remain in that building. The students were then distributed between other buildings for the remainder of the term. Some were moved into the high school.

The Central School did have annexes, and those remained in use. A letter was sent to all parents explaining the reason for the change and telling them where their child would be moved.

In order to save money, school officials did not award a bid for the work. The lowest bid received for razing the structure was $500, and it was believed it could be done for less. George Sparrow, a Civil War veteran, who was described as "one of the oldest and best contractors of the city," was assigned to get a crew together and supervise the work. Sparrow had been around when the school went up and even recalled seeing a derrick fall and damage the building.

The furniture was, of course, taken out first, and then workmen began removing the roof. Several hundred dollars' worth of scrap material was sold. Even the brick, which was still in good condition, was to be sold.

In just a few weeks, the old Central School was no more. Ten years after it was torn down, the Vincennes Coliseum (now Adams Coliseum) was built on the site.

29

Vincennes Police Department Acquires First Motorized Vehicle

In 1916, the City of Vincennes made a purchase that brought the police department into the twentieth century. That year, the department acquired its first motorized patrol wagon.

Up until that time, Vincennes patrolmen walked their beats, although three men were designated bicycle police and thus had wheels. There was a horse-drawn patrol wagon at that time, pulled by Old Charley, a former fire department horse, who had been promoted to the position.

Even the horse-drawn wagon had not been put into use until about 1904. Prior to that time, officers had the unenviable task of walking people to jail. If someone was intoxicated, but could still function, the arresting officer would lock arms with the person and head to jail, no matter the distance. If the individual couldn't walk, the officer patrolling the next beat would have to be summoned so the two could carry the person together.

It was in September of that year that department members met to decide what type of car to buy. They chose an Overland Six-cylinder model manufactured by the Willys-Overland Company of Toledo, Ohio. The chassis and engine came from Sol Allman, manager of the Gibson-Overland Company at First and Main Streets. The remainder of the car was then to be built to the specifications of the department by John Browdues, who sold auto accessories. A 1916 Overland Six sold for $1,145.

Allman loaned the department an Overland Touring car until the new car was ready. The police department also wanted two motorcycles but couldn't afford them at that time.

The new patrol wagon was turned over to the police on December 7. It was painted Brewster Green, with the words "POLICE DEPARTMENT" appearing in gold lettering on each side and "City of Vincennes" in smaller letters on the front doors. The car was housed at the A.L. Maxwell Company Garage at Fourth and Busseron Streets, which was close to police headquarters.

At that time, it was tradition in some cities for new patrol wagons to be named after the first person arrested and transported in the vehicle, but Vincennes police decided to name their car "Bobbie" after Sir Robert Peel (1788–1850). In 1829, as British home secretary, Peel had created the Metropolitan Police Force.

A trial run of the car was planned for Friday, December 8, but that turned out to be a rainy day and no one wanted to take the spanking new car out on muddy streets, so it was postponed until Monday.

Officer William Gayer drove the car, starting out at city hall at Fourth and Main Streets, and patrolman Benjamin Carr drove on the return trip. The vehicle was packed with city officials and other observers. Among the passengers were Mayor James House, Police Superintendent Harry Adams, City Engineer Harry Watts, Police Commissioners Schuyler C. Beard and John Nestlehut, Sol Allman and some newspapermen.

The reason for the trial, other than to test the car's capabilities, was to get the public used to seeing it and hearing its gong sound so they understood that they were to give it the right of way. Officers were also stationed at various points on that day to watch traffic.

The car functioned perfectly, and all agreed that it was a much-needed addition to the department.

Not long after the car was put into service, one Frank Smith, a stranger in town, had the dubious distinction of being the first person transported to jail. Smith was taken in for begging.

With the car in use, Old Charley, who had pulled the patrol wagon for so many years, enjoyed retirement on a local pasture.

30
ARNOLD'S HOBBY BROUGHT HAPPINESS TO THOUSANDS

Every day, people mail birthday, anniversary or some other type of card as a means of acknowledging a significant event in the life of a friend or loved one. Some make a true hobby out of the practice, sending countless cards every year. It is safe to say that no one has come close to the record for mailing out cards as a pastime that was established by Knox County native Allie Arnold. Over the course of a thirty-four-year period, Arnold, by his own estimation, sent an astonishing 200,000 cards, mostly for birthdays and anniversaries.

He was born Aloysius A. Arnold (but went by the name Allie) on January 4, 1889, to Stephen and Mary Memering Arnold. He married Ethel Bowling in 1916.

Over the course of his career, Arnold was a newspaper and advertising man and held elected office. He worked for four different Vincennes newspapers in a variety of capacities. Arnold was advertising manager for the Saiter-Morgan Company hardware business; was a map publisher; and served two terms as Knox County Clerk, a term as state representative for Knox County and a term as Knox County assessor. Further, he became known for his Sunday afternoon WAOV Radio broadcasts under the name *The Old Timer* and wrote the "Vincennes Vignette" and "Not So Very Long Ago" columns for the *Sun-Commercial*.

Despite his busy life, he still pursued his time-consuming hobby, the only leisure activity he had.

Allie Arnold (*seated right*) at work at his desk at the office of the *Vincennes Commercial*. Knox County Public Library's McGrady-Brockman House.

It was in September 1917 that Arnold began sending birthday and anniversary postcards as a means of spreading some cheer during the dark months of the First World War. At that time, he was working as a reporter for the *Vincennes Capital*, and part of his job was to visit families who had a son or sons in the service so that he could write about their activities. Arnold saw the fear and anxiety in those homes and decided he could do something positive to bring people he knew some joy. He also got inspiration from his parents, especially his father, who died in 1915 and had always instilled in his son the importance of having friends and of showing kindness to others.

When he was employed at the *Vincennes Commercial* in 1930, he even started a "Birthday Club" in which readers could fill out and send in a coupon and have their birthday listed in the paper. Arnold served as the birthday editor, so that is likely how he obtained many of the dates for cards he sent.

At the peak of his hobby, Arnold was sending a staggering 9,800 cards a year, eventually to nineteen states. He maintained a file to keep all of his names and dates in order but never allowed any commercial use of this valuable resource. Arnold was known for his elegant handwriting and signed each card with a unique flowing script.

Since he was involved in politics for much of his life, it is probably not surprising that political opponents would accuse the Republican Arnold of sending the cards as a means of getting votes. This issue arose in the fall of 1958 when he was seeking reelection as county assessor—a race he lost. Arnold gave a radio broadcast on October 26, absolutely refuting the claim and explaining how his hobby began. He stated that he had even sent cards to his opponent, who certainly wasn't going to vote for him. Some cards also went out of state to people who obviously wouldn't be casting local votes.

By the time of these accusations, Arnold had already discontinued his longstanding hobby. It came to an end in December 1951 due to increasing postal rates. It still cost three cents to mail a first-class letter at that time, but a postcard stamp rose from a penny to two cents on January 1, 1952. He was already spending nearly one hundred dollars a year to mail his cards—thus, the increase would double his costs. Some people he had started sending cards to back in 1917 were still receiving them. After the postal hike, he continued to send cards only to family and his closest friends.

Family and friends acknowledged Arnold's birthday too. When he turned eighty on January 4, 1969, they held a big reception for him.

During his final years, Allie Arnold lived at the Old French Towne Apartments at 600 Nicholas Street. He died at Crestview Nursing Home at the age of eighty-two on March 5, 1971. Four children survived him. His wife, Ethel, died in 1951. Burial was in Mt. Calvary Cemetery

Despite his impressive work résumé, Arnold's lasting legacy was the happiness he brought to others through his three-plus-decade-long hobby.

Ruth Jordan Served as Nurse Overseas during First World War

Women all across the country played a significant role in the First World War, not only by taking jobs in factories on the homefront but also by working as nurses, both in stateside army camps and overseas. The U.S. Army Nurse Corps was formed by Congress in 1901. By the time the armistice was signed in November 1918, there were 21,480 nurses in the corps and more than 10,000 nurses had seen service overseas. A total of 272 nurses died in the war, all from disease, including influenza.

Members of the Army Nurse Corps worked in all kinds of hospitals, from field hospitals to convalescent hospitals. Each nurse oversaw ten hospital beds.

According to the Indiana adjutant general's report, Ruth Jordan was one of five Knox County women who served in the Army Nurse Corps in World War I. The others were Anna Mae Burton, Iva P. Myers and Mary L. Wendling, all of Vincennes, and Kathleen H. McCarty of Bicknell. Other local nurses undertook work with the Red Cross.

Ruth Ellen Jordan was born in Knox County to John W. and Dorcas McKee Jordan on September 17, 1888. She had a distinguished lineage. Her maternal grandfather, Archibald Buntin McKee, was the nephew of Francis Vigo. The family lived on the former Vigo farm near Fritchton.

Jordan graduated from Good Samaritan Hospital's School of Nursing in 1915 and was first employed at the hospital. She would be the hospital's only graduate who would serve overseas during the war. Jordan joined the Army Nurse Corps and got her orders for foreign service on February 21,

Good Samaritan Hospital where Ruth Jordan spent part of her nursing career. She died at the hospital in 1950. *Knox County Public Library's McGrady-Brockman House.*

1918. She departed with a group of nurses from Anderson, Indiana. The only other Vincennes woman working as a nurse overseas at that time was Marie Burke, who had received her training in New York. Burke was a Red Cross nurse.

In mid-April, Good Samaritan Hospital superintendent Edith Willis received a postcard from Jordan saying that the former student had arrived safely overseas. In a letter dated April 12 delivered to the hospital on May 2, Jordan reported on her time in England and talked about the massive number of soldiers she was seeing. She wrote: "The nights are filled with the steady 'tramp, tramp tramp' of passing American, British and French soldiers." She had already visited Americans who were sick or wounded.

Jordan's friends had a letter from her in mid-June 1918. She was then serving at a U.S. military hospital in England. She also saw service in France.

After she came back from the war in the spring of 1919, she put her nursing skills to work in a variety of ways. She first worked as a private duty nurse. An October 1919 news item noted that Jordan was attending a newborn baby near Decker. When her father died in 1928, she was living in Louisville, Kentucky.

Jordan never married but devoted her life to nursing. She even had additional medical training as an anesthetist. When the 1930 federal census

Ruth Jordan wearing her nurse's uniform. Jordan served overseas during the First World War. *Courtesy of Good Samaritan Hospital.*

was taken, her residence was Lincoln, Nebraska, and she was working as an anesthetist at Bryan Memorial Hospital. When her mother passed away in 1934, Ruth was living at home. By 1940, she was employed as a nurse at the Knox County Infirmary. She also worked at Hillcrest Tuberculosis Hospital.

Ruth Jordan died at Good Samaritan Hospital, the place where she had long ago started her nursing career, at the age of sixty-one, on April 23, 1950. She had been suffering from a heart condition. Burial was in Fairview Cemetery. She was survived by a sister who lived in Mississippi and nieces and nephews.

The opportunities opened to them by the war helped advance women's causes. It was less than two years after the war's end, on August 18, 1920, that the Nineteenth Amendment was ratified giving women the right to vote.

32
MEN FAIL IN ATTEMPT TO ROB BRUCEVILLE STATE BANK

Robert Barr and his wife, Elizabeth, had the scare of their lives when, just after midnight on July 30, 1918, they awoke to find three armed men standing around their bed. Mr. Barr was cashier of the Bruceville State Bank, and the men intended to rob the bank by having him open the safe. A fourth man stood guard outside.

Barr immediately explained that the safe was on a time lock and couldn't be opened until morning, at which point one of the would-be robbers hit him in the head with the butt of a pistol. The terrified couple was then forced to walk to the bank—which was about a block away—barefoot and in their nightclothes. Mr. Barr was allowed to put on trousers, and they draped coats around themselves.

Once the group entered the bank, they had to get into the vault to reach the safe. The vault was secured by both an inner and an outer door, which opened by combination locks. The frightened cashier said that he had left home without his glasses and couldn't see to open the combinations. This provoked the men into further physical abuse toward him and threats against his wife's life. Barr then told them the combinations, and after several anxious moments, they got the vault doors opened. The relieved Barr was later quoted as saying that when they got into the vault it "was the happiest moment in my entire life."

The pair was then forced inside the vault as continued threats were made against them. Barr had been truthful about the safe being on a time lock. Upon the realization that it couldn't be opened, the infuriated robbers ripped strips of cloth from Mrs. Barr's nightgown and gagged the couple, also binding their hands. They then departed, stating that they would return in fifteen minutes and blow the safe, with the Barrs still in the vault.

The men did not come back to the bank, and Mr. Barr was finally able to get one hand loose and free himself and his wife. Their next task was to get out of the vault. A gate separated the safe from the vault doors, but fortunately, there was a space above the gate. Barr helped his wife over the gate and then climbed over himself. They then found themselves to be exceedingly fortunate in that the men had failed to throw the vault combination locks. They were thus able to push both doors open. They noted that by this time the air in the vault was becoming very close.

The authorities were summoned, and Knox County sheriff John Wolfe and others launched an investigation. The men had not worn masks but did have hats pulled down hiding their faces. They were described as amateurs but still dangerous. The *Bicknell Monitor* called them "amateur thugs."

No arrests were made in the case. They got only twenty or twenty-five dollars—taken from the money till—for their night's work and failed to notice some other smaller amounts.

Barr's cousin Joseph was president of the bank. He claimed that there was rarely more than $5,000 in the safe at any given time, as that sum met customers' needs. The *Vincennes Sun* reported that the safe held $65,000, but that statement was refuted by the bank.

As for Mr. and Mrs. Barr, they soon recovered from their ordeal. Mr. Barr was quite bruised. Both were badly shaken. Mrs. Barr was severely affected by the emotional trauma of the experience.

After Joseph Barr's death in 1922, Robert took over as president of the bank. Suffering from a heart condition, he died suddenly on March 14, 1931, at the age of sixty-nine while attending a basketball game at the Vincennes Coliseum. His lengthy obituary in the *Bicknell Daily News* even made mention of the attempted robbery that had occurred thirteen years earlier. Elizabeth Barr died on June 18, 1937.

The Bruceville State Bank, which was founded in 1915, closed its doors in 1943.

33

BRUNO THE BEAR MADE HIS HOME IN VINCENNES FOR MANY YEARS

Throughout the 1920s, a tame black bear named Bruno was known by every resident of Vincennes. For several years, Bruno made his home in a cage in front of a downtown department store and later lived at the Harmony Park Zoo. Bruno's story makes for an interesting bit of local history.

Bruno's tale began in November 1919. It was that month that William Farrell, of Farrell's Department Store, located on the southeast corner of First and Main Streets, purchased Bruno from a man at Carlisle who had acquired him from a traveling show. Bruno was thought to be about fifteen months old when the transaction was made.

Farrell's intention was to butcher the bear. In fact, he already had buyers for the meat and even the hide. Obviously, many local people had bear meat on their Thanksgiving menu that year. Fortunately for Bruno, there was a huge public outcry against this plan, especially among women and children. Farrell received phone calls and letters asking that Bruno's life be spared. Although he hoped that the commotion would die down and perhaps Bruno could become Christmas dinner instead, he finally relented and allowed the bear to live in a cage outside his store.

Bruno actually became a valuable addition to the Farrell store. A live bear out on the city's Main Street certainly was a unique attraction. Almost everyone who came downtown strolled to First and Main to see him. Children, naturally, became very attached to Bruno and would feed him peanuts and candy. While likely not a happy existence for the bear, at least he had not been killed and eaten.

Bruno was sometimes taken out of his cage to participate in community events. April 21, 1922, for instance, was opening day of the local baseball season, and Bruno took part in the opening day parade. On that particular day, he broke his chain at Third and Broadway Streets and roamed loose for a time, scaring quite a few people.

Bruno's fate again hung in the balance in early 1923. On January 17, Farrell's Department Store burned. The store was a total loss and would not be rebuilt. (The former store site is now part of Patrick Henry Square.) Although Bruno was in his cage when the fire broke out, the cage door was opened so the bear could escape the heat and flames. Later, Bruno was coaxed back to his cage. He was then sold to Charles B. O'Donnell, who owned several meat markets and had a big cold storage and meatpacking plant at First and Busseron Streets (where Dot's is now located).

Again, there were fears that the bear might end up on dining room tables. There were even letters to the editor published in the *Vincennes Commercial* by those concerned with Bruno's plight. One writer suggested that his cage be placed on the lawn of city hall at Fourth and Main Streets, but for the time being, it remained outside O'Donnell's meatpacking plant.

In early February 1923, O'Donnell was entertaining bids for Bruno from out-of-town buyers who wanted to display him in a public park. In March 1924, he changed his plans slightly and announced that Bruno would be donated to the Harmony Society for the small zoo it had established at Harmony Park, just east of the city.

Besides Bruno, and later a second black bear, a female named Josephine, the diverse menagerie at the park included deer, monkeys, alligators and eagles, among other animals. Many special events were held at the park over the years, including the annual Farmers' Picnic, and Bruno became a favorite of park visitors.

Bruno resided at Harmony Park through the remainder of the 1920s. As the years passed, it was noted that the aging Bruno was suffering from rheumatism.

With the onset of the Great Depression, the cost of keeping the animals at the park had become prohibitive. At its March 3, 1930 meeting, the Harmony Society voted to dispose of the animals. Some of the deer were sold that year. On April 6, 1931, a committee was appointed to facilitate removing the remaining animals, including Bruno and Josephine. On May 4, the committee reported that Evansville's Mesker Park Zoo, which had opened in 1928, would take the animals and even crate them and haul them off. Members then voted to give the animals to the zoo, and after nearly a dozen years, Bruno's time in Vincennes came to an end.

34
"CORNSTALK KILLING" FRIGHTENED THE COMMUNITY IN 1919, PART 1

On the evening of Friday, August 22, 1919, seventy-five-year-old Vincennes resident Anna Leinbach, a widow, walked from 818 Upper Eleventh Street, where she lived with her daughter Carrie Pickering, to spend some time with her son William, who was extremely ill at his home at 1129 Busseron Street. It was after dark before she began the return trip, having turned down the offer of a ride, and the family became worried as the hours passed and she did not arrive home. On that summer night, Mrs. Leinbach was the victim of one of the most heinous crimes ever to occur in the city.

It was Anna Leinbach's son-in-law, Thomas, who alerted her son Henry that his mother hadn't made it home. The police were contacted, and a search was soon initiated. Streets and alleys were combed in the darkness, with the search later suspended until daylight. It wasn't until 6:00 a.m. the next morning that the aged woman's bloodied and bruised body was discovered in a patch of tall weeds and corn in back of the Dunbar School at Twelfth and Seminary Streets. Plainclothes police officer William Blunk made the awful find. It was apparent from the scene that Mrs. Leinbach had been dragged from the street into the alley and then into a garden.

The remains were taken to Dexter Gardner & Son Funeral Home, where an autopsy was conducted. It was determined that she had been choked to death and the body then mutilated with cornstalks, hence the sobriquet "cornstalk killing" that some would attach to the crime.

The part of town where the murder occurred was known as the Idaho section and was predominately populated by African Americans. The

The Dunbar School for African American children was the site of the infamous "Cornstalk Killing" in 1919. *Views of Vincennes.*

Dunbar School was the school for African American children. Suspicion unfairly fell on several men from that neighborhood. Some were arrested but later released.

On Sunday and Monday, residents visited the site of the murder—most out of morbid curiosity—and apparently, in those days, keeping people away from the scene of a crime was not a priority.

On Monday, as the search for the killer continued, Anna Leinbach's funeral was held at St. John's Lutheran Church. The body was taken to her son William's home so he could see his mother one last time, since he was too sick to attend the service. She was also survived by son Henry and three daughters. Burial was in Fairview Cemetery.

Police continued to work the case. The only real clues found at the scene were a pipe and an empty cigarette pack. Many people in the neighborhood had reported hearing screams and other noises that night, but thought nothing of it, since they were accustomed to drunks in that area. Rumors swirled about the city, but the identity of the assailant remained a mystery for days.

Finally, on September 3, twelve days following the murder, as a result of dogged detective work, an arrest was made, although it was not immediately made public. The accused in the case was thirty-nine-year-old William A. Schutter, who lived with his wife and three children at 1024 Harrison Street. Schutter was arrested at his place of employment, the Central Foundry Company, by Superintendent Thomas Martin and Officer Blunk. It was known that Schutter had been absent from his home the night of the murder, and one of his coworkers claimed that the pipe found at the scene belonged to Schutter. Further, he had been in trouble with the law before and had a reputation for a mean temperament, especially when drinking, as had been the case on the night in question.

Although William Schutter was confined in the Knox County Jail, it was several more days before the police got a confession out of him, learning precisely what had transpired.

35

LOCAL MAN CONFESSED TO INFAMOUS MURDER, PART 2

On September 3, 1919, Vincennes police made an arrest in the Anna Leinbach murder case. Mrs. Leinbach, an aged widow, had been found strangled in a garden near the Dunbar School early on the morning of August 23. The case had remained shrouded in mystery for days, until an accumulation of evidence finally led police to believe that one William Schutter was the culprit.

Schutter was confined in the Knox County Jail, but for days he continued to claim that he had no part in the crime. Finally, early on the morning of Sunday, September 7, after nearly eleven solid hours of questioning by authorities, during which time he was even handcuffed and taken back to the scene of the crime, Schutter broke down and admitted he had murdered Mrs. Leinbach.

Schutter stated that he had been drunk on Jamaica Ginger (known as "Jake"), a highly alcoholic patent medicine, on the night of the crime. He had come upon Mrs. Leinbach by chance and said that, given his condition, any woman he encountered that night would have met the same fate. He used cornstalks to mutilate the body in order to throw police off.

Among those who witnessed the signed confession were Vincennes police superintendent Thomas Martin, patrolman William Blunk, Knox County sheriff Harry C. Adams and attorneys Curtis Shake and Joseph Kimmell.

Schutter was immediately taken to the Vigo County Jail for his own safety, where he was placed under a suicide watch. On September 9, Knox County prosecuting attorney Hugh Barr traveled there to get a second signed confession.

The grand jury convened and, on September 17, indicted Schutter on a charge of first-degree murder. Things moved quickly from that point on. The following morning, he was brought back to Vincennes and appeared in the Knox Circuit Court for arraignment. After conferring with attorney Arthur A. Clark, he entered a guilty plea and waived a jury trial. Circuit Court judge Thomas B. Coulter then sentenced Schutter to life in prison, and the convicted killer found himself on the 10:37 a.m. train bound for the Indiana State Prison in Michigan City.

There are several postscripts to the story.

Anna Leinbach's son William, whom she had visited on the night she was killed, was suffering from cancer and died on November 15 of that same year.

Schutter's wife, Alvina, obtained a divorce in the Knox Circuit Court in January 1920 and received custody of the three children. She married William Cushman on June 7, 1921. Alvina died on April 30, 1943.

Not surprisingly, given that it was such a brutal crime, Vincennes residents were opposed to any early release for Schutter and spoke out against him any time his name came up for possible parole. The opposition had not abated even thirty-five years later, when the seventy-four-year-old self-confessed murderer was finally released from prison. A headline of the May 19, 1954 edition of the *Vincennes Sun-Commercial* read simply, "William Schutter, Famous Vincennes Lifer, Paroled." It was said that Schutter had a good prison record and had even become a skilled locksmith.

William Schutter returned to Vincennes and lived at the home of one of his daughters. He died at Good Samaritan Hospital on March 18, 1958, at the age of seventy-eight. Burial was in Fairview Cemetery, the same resting place as his victim from all those years ago.

PART III
1920–1930

36
STORY FROM THE 1920s BECAME ONE OF THE MOST BIZARRE IN LOCAL HISTORY

It was one of the most bizarre, truly macabre stories in Vincennes's history, one that even today reads more like fiction than fact.

It all began on February 3, 1920, when a woman named Rosa Gillenwaters died at the age of thirty-six in Wichita, Kansas. Gillenwaters's body was embalmed, and her husband, Frank, was attempting to transport it to South Bend, Indiana, for interment there. Frank Gillenwaters was an entertainer and traveled from town to town with his stepdaughters doing musical acts.

He had passed through several communities with his wife's remains, which were supposedly first contained in a basket, before he was required by officials to get a casket. He arrived in Vincennes by train on October 5, 1920, eight months after Rosa's death, having come from Cairo, Illinois. The body was immediately removed to Dexter Gardner & Son Funeral Home, where it was placed in the business's crypt. While in town, Frank and his girls performed at the Moon Theater on Main Street, next door to the funeral home.

Gillenwaters, who claimed he didn't presently have the money to take the body any further, was given permission by Gardner's to temporarily leave the remains in its crypt, with the agreement that he pay fifty cents a week for storage. With this arrangement made, he left town.

Oddly enough, as news of this morbid story spread, townspeople came to the funeral home just to see the body, which was said to be a "rare sample of expert embalming." In fact, Gillenwaters had shown it in other cities.

Above: The Gardner Funeral Home on Main Street in 1915. The body of Rosa Gillenwaters remained unclaimed there for a decade. *Views of Vincennes.*

Left: Rosa Gillenwaters's monument in Vincennes's Fairview Cemetery. *Author's collection.*

In December 1921, Frank Gillenwaters was arrested in West Frankfort, Illinois, and served a lengthy term in the Leavenworth Penitentiary. It seems that his relationship with his wife's daughters from a previous marriage was morally and legally wrong. He had been charged with and convicted of violating the Mann Act, which passed in 1910, making it illegal to transport women across state lines for immoral purposes.

The weeks turned into months and the months into years and Rosa Gillenwaters's body languished in Vincennes, with no word from her husband. No one even knew if he was dead or alive, but obviously, the situation needed to be resolved.

Finally, a full decade later, in July 1930, word was received that Frank Gillenwaters was confined in an insane asylum in Washington, D.C.

Funeral director Dexter Gardner then wrote to Gillenwaters, who responded with his own letter, asking that his wife's remains be buried in Vincennes, on "dry and high ground so that she would not have a watery grave." He also asked that the grave be marked. Parts of his letter were coherent, and parts were not.

The funeral home first had to get permission from the Indiana State Board of Health but was finally able to inter the body. Rosa Gillenwaters's burial was in Fairview Cemetery on August 12, with Pastor Charles Whitman of the First Methodist Episcopal Church in charge of a very short service.

Thus, ten years after it began, this strange series of events reached its conclusion. Today, only a few old newspaper articles, funeral home records and a stone in Fairview Cemetery allow the story to be pieced together.

37

Franklin Roosevelt Spoke to Voters at the Knox County Courthouse

On the morning of Thursday, October 14, 1920, a crowd estimated at 1,200 strong gathered on the Eighth Street side of the Knox County Courthouse to hear a national figure make a campaign speech. The program was set to begin at 11:00 a.m., but the speaker was running behind schedule. To keep people entertained prior to the candidate's arrival, Arthur Balue's First Regiment Band played some tunes and local attorney John Riddle gave a talk.

Finally, at around 11:25 a.m., the man the crowd had assembled to hear, Franklin D. Roosevelt, mounted a platform to deliver his speech.

The thirty-eight-year-old Roosevelt, who had served as assistant secretary of the navy in Woodrow Wilson's administration, was the vice-presidential nominee on the Democratic ticket with Ohio governor James Cox. Cox and Roosevelt were opposed by the Republican ticket of Ohio senator Warren G. Harding and his running mate, Calvin Coolidge, governor of Massachusetts. While Harding waged a "front porch" campaign from his Ohio home, the Democratic team was out campaigning across the country.

Roosevelt, along with his wife, Eleanor, and a small entourage, was traveling by automobile. He came to Vincennes following an appearance in Sullivan and then proceeded to Princeton and Evansville.

Roosevelt was introduced by Mary Kapps, who chaired the Women's Division of the Knox County Democratic Central Committee. Besides the expected criticism of Harding, his speech focused in a large part on the Democrat's endorsement of the League of Nations, the international post–

Franklin Roosevelt campaigning in 1920 as the vice-presidential candidate on the ticket with James Cox. Roosevelt's appearance in Vincennes would have looked much like this photo.
Library of Congress, Prints and Photographs Division, Washington, D.C.

World War I organization aimed at maintaining the peace, which the U.S. Senate had failed to ratify. His speech concluded at noon.

Typically, the extremely partisan newspapers of the day had different takes on the candidates' appearance. Of Roosevelt, the Democrat-leaning *Vincennes Sun* commented, "He is a wonderful speaker and presents the Democratic message in a most convincing manner." The paper went on to say, "A large crowd heard the distinguished visitor."

The Republican *Vincennes Commercial*, on the other hand, was critical of Roosevelt's speech and said that, even though Democrats placed the crowd at 1,200, that number was much lower than what had been expected. The paper also claimed that many curious Republicans had turned out.

Following his speech, Roosevelt was taken to the Grand Hotel for lunch. Members of the Daughters of the American Revolution took Eleanor Roosevelt to a luncheon at the First Methodist Episcopal Church. Vincennes was filled with DAR women, since their state conference was currently underway in the city.

The Republicans trounced the Democrats in the November election. Harding was elected president with 16,147,249 votes to Cox's 9,140,864. The electoral vote totaled 404 to 127.

Harding carried Knox County 10,011 votes to 8,052 votes for Cox. The Socialist candidate Eugene V. Debs received 919 votes in the county.

Of course, when Franklin Roosevelt visited Vincennes in 1920, he walked across the courthouse lawn and stepped up on to the platform on his own. It was the following year, in August 1921, that he contracted polio, resulting in paralysis.

Roosevelt visited Vincennes again in June 1936, this time as president, to dedicate the George Rogers Clark Memorial.

38

CHECKERS CHAMP BANKS COMPETED IN VINCENNES

Today, the name Newell W. Banks is unknown to most people, except perhaps checkers and chess enthusiasts, but Banks, a Detroit native, was considered the best American checkers player of his day, perhaps of all time. In fact, he was a world champion. Newell Banks demonstrated his amazing skills in Vincennes on more than one occasion. One of those times was in November 1920, when he came to the city to play local checkers champs.

Many people enjoyed playing checkers in those years. The local YMCA organized a checkers club and held a couple of tournaments. As the *Vincennes Commercial* stated in its May 3, 1919 edition: "Checkers has become a popular game at the 'Y,' and anyone interested in the game will always find someone there to take them on."

On Saturday evening, November 27, Banks played checkers at the YMCA Gymnasium. (The YMCA was then located at Fourth and Broadway Streets.) The then thirty-three-year-old Banks was on a tour of the United States at the time.

Admission was twenty-five cents for spectators, and there was a registration fee of fifty cents for players who wanted to compete against the champ. These costs paid Banks's expenses.

Banks had two unique skills, both of which he demonstrated during play at the YMCA. First, he was able to play multiple games of checkers simultaneously. What created even more drama and astonished onlookers was that Banks could play checkers successfully while blindfolded. In blindfolded games, players did not see or touch the checkers but rather spoke the moves to a third person and then were required to remember the location of the pieces. Needless to say, that form of play took great mental acuity. What was even more impressive was the fact that Banks could play numerous blindfolded games simultaneously.

Banks also was a skilled chess player, said to be one of very few people who excelled at both checkers and chess. He played chess blindfolded as well.

Many good local players challenged Banks. Around twelve men played him in the simultaneous games and a half dozen in the blindfolded games. The last time Banks had been in Vincennes, Elmer Johnson, of rural Decker, had three draws out of nine games. Johnson didn't do quite as well against the champ during that November visit. That time, he got one draw, as did Jack Turrell of Vincennes. Turrell achieved his draw in one of the blindfolded games.

It was a fun time for all, not only for those who came to see some phenomenal play but especially for those who got to take on the man considered the best checkers player in America.

Newell Banks demonstrated his skill at checkers while a boy, playing his first blindfolded game at a young age. He was considered a child prodigy and continued to develop his game and expertise. He won the United States Checkers Championship in 1907. In 1922, he competed against Robert Stewart in Glasgow, Scotland, for the title of world champion. Stewart was the top checkers player in Europe. (The game of checkers was actually called draughts in Britain.) He lost that match to Stewart but went on to win the title of world champion in 1934.

Checkers champion Newell Banks died in Detroit at the age of eighty-nine on February 17, 1977.

39

OLD POST LAUNDRY WAS AN INNOVATION FOR VINCENNES

It was the year 1902 that Dr. Gottlieb A. Pielemeier became the first auto owner in Vincennes when he purchased a primitive Oldsmobile. Of course, as more and more people acquired automobiles, businesses associated with their maintenance sprang up. Besides auto dealers, there were, naturally, those who specialized in accessories, tires and repairs. Eventually, the now ubiquitous filling station evolved. The first true filling station in Vincennes opened on the corner of Fourth and Busseron Streets in 1918.

One other need of auto owners, especially since there were still so many unpaved streets, was the car wash. The first car wash in the United States opened, not surprisingly, in Detroit, in 1914. That car wash was not automated; rather, the cars were pushed through and washed and dried by hand, although it was still called an "Automated Laundry." It was not until decades later that car washes would be completely automated. Further, the term "car wash" was not used in those years; rather "Automobile Laundries" is typically how a place where one had one's car washed was described.

It was the funeral home Dexter Gardner & Son, then operated by George and Dexter Gardner, that established the first car wash in Vincennes. In 1921, the Gardners opened what was quaintly termed the Old Post Auto Laundry. The auto laundry was in the Gardner garage at Fourth and Dubois Streets, in a forty-by-eighty-foot space with a concrete floor. That part of the garage had once been used for stabling horses before the funeral business was motorized.

It was in late April of that year that Gardners announced that they would soon be opening an auto laundry. The *Vincennes Commercial* welcomed the news, writing in the April 28 edition: "The announcement of the opening of the Auto Laundry will be hailed with delight by the auto owners of the city, as well as the traveling public, as such an institution devoted exclusively to this line has been a crying necessity in the city for some time."

The Old Post Auto Laundry had its official opening, with demonstrations from 10:00 a.m. to noon on Wednesday, June 22, 1921. Their newspaper ad for the event read in part: "Have Your Automobile Laundered in Latest Scientific Manner, Including Upholstering Cleaned By Our ARCO WAND VACUUM CLEANER."

In order to draw a crowd, the First Regiment Band departed from the corner of Third and Main Streets at 9:00 a.m. that day and marched to the laundry, where they gave a concert.

Hundreds of people turned out to see the auto laundry, and the first ten cars were washed for free.

The process was fairly simple, although novel for the time. The interior of a car was first gone over with the vacuum cleaner. The vehicle was then placed on a rack and thoroughly soaked with water. A large water pipe had been installed so as to get greater pressure and thus remove more dirt. The next step was to use multiple hoses and clean the car with soap and water. Several men did all of this work. Lastly, the auto was moved to an area where it was dried off and shined. Women were employed for those final steps.

It was said that a car could be washed in twenty-five minutes, and it was expected that that time could eventually be slashed to fifteen minutes. Unfortunately, no accounts of the opening of the Old Post Auto Laundry reveal how much it cost to have one's car "laundered."

Vincennes City Directories show that the next business in town to offer automobile washing, also in the 1920s, was the East End Garage at Fairground (now Washington) and Ridgeway Avenues, operated by Thomas L. Brouillette.

40
St. Louis Cardinals Played the Bicknell Braves

On the afternoon of July 25, 1921, Bicknell baseball fans had their eyes trained on the skies, watching as ominous rain clouds rolled in. After a prolonged dry spell, rain should have been welcome, but on that afternoon, the big-league St. Louis Cardinals were to be in town for an exhibition game with the hometown Bicknell Braves, so rain was the last thing that game organizers wanted.

The deal for the Cardinals' appearance had been finalized on July 19. The signed contract guaranteed that the team would field the regular lineup, including star batter (and future Hall of Famer) Rogers Hornsby. The Cardinals were paid $1,000.

An enormous out-of-town crowd was expected for the game. Additional bleachers were to be built at North Side Park so fewer people would have to stand. A special train was arranged so that fans traveling from the northeast could return home the same day.

While game day began clear, by the noon hour, it was sprinkling rain. Play was scheduled to begin at 4:00 p.m., but just after 2:00 p.m. the sky grew dark and an hour later a steady rain began. There were already hundreds of people in the park and many more waiting in their cars.

The Cardinals, traveling between New York and St. Louis, arrived at about 3:30 p.m., coming from Indianapolis in a Pullman car. By that time, it was questionable as to whether the game could be played on the muddy grounds. Finally, another shower of about a half hour's duration forced its cancellation.

Fortunately, the Bicknell committee that had organized the exhibition game had wisely taken out an insurance policy in the event of a rain out. The group paid $140 for a $1,000 policy.

The game between the Bicknell Braves and the St. Louis Cardinals was rescheduled for September 7 at 3:00 p.m., what turned out to be a day of fine weather. The Cardinals came back to town, this time directly from St. Louis, where they had just beaten the Chicago Cubs in a double header.

The game drew a huge crowd. An estimated two to three thousand people turned out.

Bicknell was said to field one of the best local teams around. The Braves' manager was Gerald Landis. Thomas Dunlap, who had played ball for other teams, was one exceptional player. He resided in Bicknell until his death in 1969 at the age of eighty.

The Braves outplayed the Cardinals, scoring six runs in the fourth inning. Hornsby batted four times but didn't get a hit, even striking out his last time at bat. The only homer was hit by Emmett Perkins, a Greene County man on the Bicknell team.

The game was finally called at the end of the eighth inning—so the Cardinals could make their 5:36 train—with Bicknell pulling off an upset of the big-league team with a final score of nine to six. It was said to be the first time the Cardinals had lost an exhibition game since 1919.

There was some speculation that the Cardinals had let the Braves win, but others believed that the Cardinals had started off easy, then realized they had a tougher opponent than they expected, by which time it was too late to recover.

The Cardinals did have one small consolation. The ladies of the Bicknell Baptist Church sent team members on their way with a hearty meal of fried chicken, cake, pie and other good food.

41

Fox Drives Were Once an Important Part of Rural Life

For many years, fox drives were an important part of rural life in Knox County. The purpose of the drives was to rid farmers of foxes that preyed on their chickens and even took young pigs. They also had a social aspect, with men, women and children taking part in a community event that had a common purpose. Local churches sold food to the participants, and the dead foxes were auctioned, with proceeds going to a charitable cause. Still, the drives were not without their critics, with some objecting to the cruelty of such an undertaking.

Fox drives could encompass one or more townships or parts of townships and involved thousands of people, requiring expert organization and coordination. Long lines were formed with people spaced at close intervals, all converging upon an agreed-on point. People made their way over rough, frozen ground and across fences, ditches, hills and streams, all the while making noise and swinging clubs to flush foxes from their dens. Teams were led by designated captains. The captains were on horseback to help keep order. No guns or dogs were allowed, and farmers were instructed to keep their stock penned up. Any unfortunate foxes that were trapped within the lines at the end of the drive, termed the "roundup," were clubbed to death.

A number of fox drives were held in Knox County during the winter of 1921–22. Two big drives were staged in the final days of 1921. The first, on December 27, rescheduled from an earlier date due to rain, was in Johnson and Harrison Townships. A blast of dynamite was the signal for the estimated three thousand people who turned out to begin moving.

By midday, thousands of acres had been covered, with the roundup on the Henry Dreiman farm in Harrison Township. Eight foxes and quite a few rabbits were corralled. Young boys were allowed to move in and club the animals. Both foxes and rabbits were then auctioned from a wagon, the money going to the Farmers' Federations of the two townships. The price each fox brought ranged from $7.50 to $11.75.

The ladies of the Iona Church sold soup, sandwiches and coffee to the hungry crowd, and there was a program of speakers. Uncle Joe Roseman, one of the county's popular Civil War veterans, was on hand to play his fife.

On the last day of that year, December 31, Vigo and Widner Townships had a fox drive, with estimates of anywhere from 1,000 to 1,500 people participating. On that morning, twelve foxes (often referred to as big red Reynards) were flushed from their dens, and nine were dispatched, along with thirty-two rabbits. The roundup took place midway between Freelandville and Edwardsport. Some people waited in their automobiles out of the cold and then jumped out to be in on the kill. The auction netted a little over one hundred dollars, which went to charity.

Busseron Township conducted a fox drive on January 7, 1922. Nine foxes were killed, but a number of others escaped through the lines. At the roundup, on the farm of Frank McClure, an angry bobcat was found to have been encircled. The animal was allowed to break free, since no one was willing to stand in its way. Around one hundred dollars was raised for charity.

On January 21, Palmyra and Washington Townships staged a fox drive. Snow lay on the ground for that drive, making conditions somewhat unpleasant. Although quite a few foxes escaped, six were killed and $49.75 was realized through the auction, that money going to the Salvation Army. The ladies of the Royal Oak Presbyterian Church sold lunch.

There were three more fox drives in Knox County that winter. On January 14, Widner Township had a drive in which five foxes were killed and $53.50 raised.

Busseron Township and Haddon Township in Sullivan County collaborated on a drive on January 28, with just two foxes killed, and on February 4, a drive in the vicinity of Bruceville ended in the deaths of three foxes.

The drives angered some people. The *Bicknell Daily News* had several letters from those who objected to their cruelty. Still, they continued in later years, as farmers considered them necessary to keep the fox population under control.

42

President Warren Harding Passed through Knox County

It was Thursday, June 21, 1923, the official start of the summer season, and Vincennes residents were already sweltering through a miserable stretch of days with ninety-plus-degree temperatures. On that day, as the sun bore down and the mercury climbed toward ninety-nine degrees, a crowd assembled at Union Depot to greet an important visitor. Those who gathered were waiting to see President Warren Harding and his wife, Florence, whose train would be making a brief late morning stop in the city.

When the train entered Knox County on the Baltimore and Ohio Railroad, it first passed through Wheatland, where its speed was slowed so those standing at crossings could wave at the president. At Washington, in Daviess County, some 750 people had been at the depot to catch a glimpse of Harding.

At 10:55 a.m., the presidential train pulled into the Vincennes depot, and people quickly surrounded the rear platform where the Hardings stood waving and smiling. Harding and his entourage were on route to the West Coast and Alaska. Vincennes was not an official stop on their itinerary—rather, the train was in the city just long enough to take on ice and water. It was Harding's first time in Vincennes as president. In 1920, while seeking to capture the Republican presidential nomination, he made a speech at the Knox County Courthouse.

Harding, hatless and dressed in what was described as "a gray business suit of conservative cut," asked the crowd if they would rather he shake hands or speak, and he ended up doing both.

In very informal remarks, he mentioned the fields of wheat he had seen and the important role of farmers in the nation's economy. He went on to

Warren and Florence Harding circa 1920. The couple made a stop in Vincennes in 1923. *Library of Congress, Prints and Photographs Division, Washington, D.C.*

say how pleased he was to see so many people and that he envied them the freedom of responsibility of the presidency. A woman had handed Florence Harding a fan, and the first lady fanned her husband as he spoke.

In describing the couple, the *Vincennes Commercial* commented: "The manner of both President and Mrs. Harding was characterized by wholesome friendliness and lack of formality." Following his short talk, Harding stepped from the train and began shaking hands.

No reporters covering the event made an estimate of the number of people who turned out.

At 11:15 a.m., just twenty minutes after it arrived, the train was again on the move.

On August 2, just weeks after local people had an opportunity to see Harding, the president died of a heart attack in San Francisco. The train returning his body east did not pass through Knox County but took a route through the northern part of Indiana. On August 10, the day of Harding's funeral, there was a special memorial service at Vincennes's Pantheon Theater, as well as services at local churches and at Vincennes University.

Vice-President Calvin Coolidge succeeded Harding, and scandals that had plagued the now deceased president's administration soon came to light, effectively destroying Harding's reputation.

43

EDWARDSPORT BANK CASHIER MURDERED IN ATTEMPTED ROBBERY, PART 1

At around 1:00 p.m. on Thursday, November 8, 1923, two men in a new Ford coupe drove into the town of Edwardsport and parked across the street from the bank. The pair went into a nearby store, where one man bought a pack of cigarettes. They then entered the bank and encountered fifty-five-year-old Charles Wright, who had just come back from lunch and was cutting kindling for the stove. Wright was filling in as cashier in place of A.B. Rich while Rich was in Vincennes picking up the miners' payroll.

One of the men pointed a gun at Wright, a .32-caliber automatic, and told him to put his hands up. This caused Wright to cry out and reach toward a money drawer. The man responded by shooting Wright twice, once in the face and once in the chest. The would-be robbers then quickly left, empty-handed, since all of the bank's money was locked in the safe. As they departed, they fired shots at Wesley Wheat and Lee Simonson, who were on a nearby farm wagon. Other men also found bullets flying their way, including Dr. John Scudder, who had emerged from his office at the rear of the bank. Dr. Scudder jumped in his car and briefly followed the men, then returned to give what medical assistance he could to Wright, who died at the scene.

The bank was near the Edwardsport School, and students in their classrooms heard the shots fired and watched the men flee.

A crowd quickly formed around the bank, law enforcement was notified, and locals went in pursuit of the men. Three men were mistakenly arrested and later released. The true culprits, Ted Armstrong and William Jones, both coal miners, were caught a short time later in Bicknell. They had blown a tire as they made their escape, so they arrived in town with one wheel missing a tire. The two bought a quart of white mule whiskey from a bootlegger prior to the attempted robbery and were still intoxicated. These were factors that initially made them suspects.

The men were taken to the Vincennes City Hall, where they were questioned intently for hours. The following morning, twenty-four-year-old Ted Armstrong finally admitted that he had fired the fatal shots and made a signed confession. Jones, who was in his mid-thirties, held out longer, but upon learning of Armstrong's confession and fearing a lynch mob, he also confessed, a confession he would later deny.

Besides the confidence gained from the whiskey, one of the principal things motivating the actions of the men was their knowledge that on July 16 the same bank had been robbed of over $2,000 (A.B. Rich was on duty that day) and those thieves had never been caught.

Since a crowd had gathered around the jail, Knox County sheriff Roy Chambers took the accused out of the county, just as a precaution. Publicly, it was stated that they were transported to Evansville, but in truth, they were taken to Washington. They were back in the Knox County Jail just a short time later.

Wright's funeral was held at Edwardsport on November 11. The victim was a widower with grown children and had lived with his daughter. He had been well known locally, having been a writer for the *Bicknell Daily News*. His present occupation was insurance agent. The town was described as being jammed with automobiles, and literally hundreds of people filed past the coffin at the home. Burial was in the Edwardsport Oddfellows Cemetery.

On November 15, a grand jury indicted Armstrong and Jones on a charge of first-degree murder. That night, a group of northern Knox County people assembled at the jail, and although the crowd was peaceful, the sheriff again took the prisoners out of the county for their own safety, this time to the Vigo County Jail.

Before the murder trial started, the July 16 bank robbery that had spurred the men on to commit their own crime was solved. On November 15, Ervin Nicholson was arrested in Georgia. A day later, Paul Hardesty was picked up in North Dakota. Both men were returned to Knox County for trial. Each entered a guilty plea in the Knox Circuit Court. On November 23, Judge Thomas Coulter sentenced them to not less than ten and not more than twenty years in the Indiana State Reformatory at Pendleton and fined them each $1,000, plus court costs.

Murdered bank cashier Charles Wright's monument in the Edwardsport IOOF Cemetery. *Author's collection.*

On December 17, Armstrong and Jones were in court to enter their respective pleas. Armstrong refused to make a plea, so the court entered a plea of not guilty. A plea of not guilty was also entered for Jones. Their trial date was set for January 15.

44

ACCUSED MURDERERS BROUGHT TO JUSTICE, PART 2

On November 15, 1923, a Knox County grand jury indicted Ted Armstrong and William Jones on a charge of first-degree murder. The pair was accused of killing Charles Wright in a failed robbery attempt of the Edwardsport Bank on November 8. On December 17, not guilty pleas were entered for both men in the Knox Circuit Court, and a trial date was set for January 15, 1924.

The court had appointed local attorney Ewing Emison to represent Armstrong, while Jones employed Felix Blankenbaker, a criminal defense attorney from Terre Haute.

Before the two men made their next court appearance, the fate of another man who had been involved in the crime was decided. On January 8, Goebel Head, from Bicknell, entered a plea of guilty in the Knox Circuit Court on a charge of conspiracy to commit a felony, having played a role in the attempted bank robbery and an earlier theft. Head, who had been arrested in Detroit in November, was to have been in on the Edwardsport robbery with Armstrong and Jones but was being held in jail on another matter when the crime took place. It was also learned that he had been involved in a July 16 robbery of the Edwardsport Bank, having aided the actual thieves in their getaway after they ditched their car. Judge Thomas B. Coulter sentenced Head to from two to fourteen years in the Indiana State Reformatory.

On January 9, Armstrong and Jones appeared, handcuffed, before Judge Coulter, at which time the judge granted Jones's request for a change of venue. His trial was moved to Greene County, and he was transferred to

Bloomfield a few days later. Armstrong, who had already confessed to the murder, changed his plea from not guilty to guilty.

On Monday, January 14, Judge Coulter sentenced Armstrong to life in the Indiana State Prison at Michigan City. The only thing that saved him from the electric chair was the statement of Dr. George Smith, a Bicknell physician, who claimed that Armstrong had a diminished mental capacity at the time the crime was committed.

Jones's trial in the Greene County Circuit Court was set for February 25. The case against him was brought by Knox County prosecuting attorney Floyd Young and two former prosecutors: Joseph Kimmell, representing the Indiana Bankers Association, and D. Frank Culbertson. These men assisted Greene County prosecutor George Humphreys. The prosecution was asking for the death penalty. Kimmell, who would go on to serve two terms as Vincennes mayor, played a big role in the case.

Jones had a new attorney by the time his trial started. Will R. Vosloh, a former Greene County prosecutor, was appointed by the court to represent him. The courtroom was completely full, many Knox County people having taken the train to Bloomfield to attend.

Oddly enough, no autopsy had been conducted on Wright's body prior to his burial, so, at the request of the prosecution, Judge Coulter ordered an exhumation. That took place on February 24, principally as a means of verifying that the bullets used had come from Armstrong's gun.

The prosecution called a slew of witnesses to make their case, but it was a defense witness who garnered the most attention. On February 27, Ted Armstrong, who had been transported back from Michigan City, testified. Although there was some difference of opinion as to his effectiveness as a witness, it was generally believed that he aided Jones's case by taking responsibility for the crime. Some observers even felt that Jones might be acquitted.

The following day, momentum swung back to the prosecution, when the defense put Jones on the stand. It was agreed by all that he made a poor showing, contradicting himself on numerous points. Even worse, it was said that during his testimony he displayed a "brazen attitude" that did not go over well with the jury.

Still, some were predicting a hung jury when they finally got the case at 3:15 p.m. on Friday, February 29.

The following morning, the jury came back with a guilty verdict and recommended a sentence of life in prison. On March 3, the Greene County judge concurred and passed the sentence of life in the Indiana State Prison. Jones, who had a wife and two children, was taken there the following day.

45
"Gentleman Jim" Made a Brief Stop at Union Depot

At just after midnight on Thursday, March 8, 1928, a sixty-one-year-old man stepped from the train at Vincennes's Union Depot and walked up to the ticket office to ask about a connecting train that would take him to Columbus, Ohio. On duty at the office was night ticket agent Pearl Cross, who immediately recognized the visitor as Jim Corbett, former world heavyweight champion.

Today, Corbett's name is likely unfamiliar to most people, but in 1928, although long retired, he remained one of the most famous men in the country, as evidenced by the fact that even his very brief late-night stop in Vincennes would generate some excitement.

James John Corbett was born in San Francisco on September 1, 1866. He had a middle-class upbringing and was quite educated. He learned to box in sparring clubs rather than out on the street. The handsome six-foot, one-inch Corbett, nicknamed "Gentleman Jim," began boxing professionally in 1886 and had many successful fights. On September 7, 1892, he won the heavyweight title when he fought John L. Sullivan at the Olympic Club in New Orleans. Corbett knocked out Sullivan in the twenty-first round. This was said to be the first such championship won using the Marquess of Queensberry Rules, which included the wearing of boxing gloves.

Corbett would come to be known as the "Father of Modern Boxing" because he helped transform the sport from a no-holds-barred brawl to more of a scientific art form.

Corbett defended his championship title in 1894, knocking out opponent Charley Mitchell in the third round of their fight. He finally lost the title to Bob Fitzsimmons in a fight at Carson City, Nevada, on March 17, 1897. Fitzsimmons scored a knockout in the fourteenth round. Corbett continued to box. He also did some acting on stage and in film, both during his time as a boxer and after retirement.

When ticket agent Cross realized it was the famed boxer at the depot, he quickly alerted several friends, who, despite the late hour, came out to meet him. They all came to the Union Depot Hotel Café and visited with Corbett for a couple of hours while he waited for his connecting train.

Those who gathered at the café were D. Frank Culbertson, of the Indiana George Rogers Clark Memorial Commission; Harry Chaney, who managed the hotel; Howard B. Houghton, a *Vincennes Commercial* reporter; *Commercial* employee Walter Hermann; and F. Albert Reiman. Reiman was a sportswriter for the *Commercial*, and the next day's edition contained a front-page story about the surprise visit. Also present was Charles L. Kuhn, composing room foreman at the *Commercial*, who had actually seen Corbett win the title back in 1892.

The men asked Corbett lots of questions, and he reminisced a bit about his boxing career. They told him about the big George Rogers Clark Sesquicentennial celebration to take place in the city in 1929, and Corbett commented, "Clark was a great man, and I hope you pay great honor to his name."

They described the former champ as being in excellent physical shape, with no gray hair. In fact, it was said he looked more like a man of fifty. He was even the same weight—190 pounds—that he had been in his fighting days.

Jim Corbett died at the age of sixty-six, in Long Island, New York, on February 18, 1933. His autobiography was made into the 1942 movie *Gentleman Jim*, with Errol Flynn in the title role.

46
LOCAL STUDENTS TOOK PART IN SPELLING BEES

In the late winter and early spring of 1928, Knox County schools were conducting spelling bees to determine a winner who would go on to compete in the Indiana Spelling Bee at Indianapolis. The state winner would then travel to Washington, D.C., for the National Spelling Bee. This was the first year that schools in Knox County participated.

It was newspapers that sponsored the spelling bees. In 1925, the *Louisville Courier-Journal* and other papers started the National Spelling Bee. The Scripps-Howard Company (later E.W. Scripps Company) became the sponsor starting in 1941, and it became known as the Scripps Howard National Spelling Bee. Today, it is simply called the Scripps National Spelling Bee. In 1928, the state sponsor in Indiana was the *Indianapolis Times*.

The *Vincennes Commercial*, under general manager Chester Adams, along with county superintendent of schools George Graham, were sponsors in Knox County. Students in grades five through eight, in both public and parochial schools, were eligible to take part.

The first round in Knox County took place on March 9, when a champion was chosen from each schoolroom. That round could be either oral or written. Teachers could even select the winner based on the student's grades. The remainder of the competition was oral only.

The second round was on March 16; the room champions competed, and a winner was chosen from each building.

Then, on the evening of Thursday, March 29, the countywide spelling bee was held at the George Rogers Clark building, and the twenty-eight building winners faced off. E.C. Cunningham, superintendent of the Lawrence County Schools, gave the words, and local attorney Hamet Hinkle served as judge. More than three hundred people turned out to watch.

Gradually, the students were eliminated, and around 1,160 words were spelled. *Experiment*, *hymn*, *seize* and *exquisite* were just some of the words that tripped up participants.

Finally, the contest was down to two spellers: Elgin Sager, a seventh grader at Gibault, and Norma Jane Huber, a sixth grader at Sacred Heart. The back and forth continued for nearly 150 words until Huber misspelled the word *tenement*. Sager, the son of Benjamin F. and Ella Sager, of Vincennes, thus became the Knox County champ.

As the winner, Sager received a $25.00 Elgin wristwatch, donated by the *Commercial*. Students at his school gave him a fountain pen and a gold pencil. Huber, as runner-up, received a *Funk & Wagnalls Dictionary*, valued at $7.50, given by Vincennes Office Equipment Company. Audria Unger, an eighth grader at Emison, placed third and won a $5.00 fountain pen donated by Leo Simon. Eloise Bond, an Oaktown eighth grader, was fourth in the competition and received a $2.50 Kodak Brownie Camera from Duesterberg & Kramer Drugstore. Fifth place went to Ralph Knox Heinekamp, who was in eighth grade at Clark School. For his efforts, Heinekamp got a $3.00 pocketknife from Walker Hardware Company.

As Knox County champion, Elgin Sager went to compete in the State Spelling Bee at Indianapolis on May 4. The *Commercial* paid his way, and one of his teachers traveled with him on the train. Forty students from Gibault gave him a sendoff at the depot.

Thirty-two spellers from across the state took part. After close to three thousand words were given, it came down to Sager and a girl from Clay County. Sager finally misspelled the word *indispensable*, which he spelled "indispensible." Second place in the state was still impressive, but Sager missed out on his chance to compete in the National Spelling Bee later that month.

The Scripps National Spelling Bee remains a popular event to this day. It has been held every year since 1925, with the exception of the war years of 1943–45. In recent years, it has been broadcast live on ESPN.

PART IV
1930–1940

47
Cooking Schools Were Once Held in Vincennes

While cooking schools are still held today, it was in the period preceding the Second World War that they were at their peak of popularity. In those days, homemaking was the principal pursuit of women until the war took many out of the home.

The purpose of the schools was to teach better cooking and housekeeping skills.

Local newspapers organized the cooking schools. One of the *Vincennes Sun-Commercial*'s predecessors, the *Vincennes Commercial*, held what would be the first of many cooking schools over four days in the winter of 1930, from February 4 through February 7. The free school took place at the Pantheon Theater at Fifth and Main Streets. Doors opened at 1:00 p.m. each day, and the sessions began at 2:00. Nationally known home economics expert Edna Ferguson conducted the school.

Hundreds of women (and just a handful of men) from Vincennes and the surrounding area turned out for the school. Some waited at the door far in advance of opening time in order to obtain the best seats. More than eight hundred attended on the first day, and the number only increased on the following days. Music from a Majestic Radio provided by Schultheis & Sons Furniture played as the women took their seats.

Nellie Coulter, wife of Knox County circuit court Judge Thomas B. Coulter, opened the first session and introduced Edna Ferguson.

All types of recipes were demonstrated by Ferguson and her assistant. On the first day alone, they showed attendees how to make cabbage soup, deviled oysters, cranberry sauce, stuffed spareribs, potato puffs, cheese crackers and balls, ham rolls, chocolate eclairs, quick sponge cake and peanut brittle. Also on the program was "Essentials in Making Good Tea." All audience members received printed copies of the recipes.

There were many other kitchen topics covered as well. Ferguson talked about marketing, budgets, diets, scientific food buying, menu planning, balanced meals, labor-saving devices and much more. Those planning to attend the classes were encouraged to bring pencil and paper for note taking. They could also submit written questions.

In its February 6 edition, the *Commercial* described the benefits of the cooking school this way: "Cookery and housework were lifted by Miss Ferguson from the realm of tiresome and unromantic drudgery into an enjoyable and instructive revelation as to possibilities of new foods, new recipes, new methods and new appliances."

The women could go up on the stage after all of the demonstrations concluded to look over the food and appliances.

Audience members received all kinds of gifts. Six big market baskets filled with food products were given away through a drawing at each session, and the prepared food items also went to people in the crowd.

Larger gifts that would be given on the final day of the school were on display. One of the most coveted was a damask tablecloth and napkins donated by H. Brokhage & Sons. Everything used for the school—including the food products, appliances, flowers and linens—were supplied by local businesses, all of which used the occasion to promote their merchandise.

Cooking schools would be sponsored in Vincennes for many more years and were always guaranteed to draw big crowds.

48
Miniature Golf Was a Popular Pastime Locally Beginning in 1930

Miniature golf was a fad that gained popularity in the late 1920s. In 1922, Thomas McCulloch Fairbairn, using crushed cottonseed hulls, oil and green dye on a sand base, created and patented an ideal surface for playing miniature golf. In 1927, Garnet Carter patented a miniature golf game called "Tom Thumb Golf," which he franchised. In 1932, Carter, a skilled promoter, opened the tourist attraction Rock City at Lookout Mountain, Georgia.

It was in 1930 that the miniature golf craze really hit locally. By that summer, there were four miniature golf courses in Vincennes and at least one out in the county. The Vincennes courses were the Kum-Back at Thirteenth and Willow Streets; the Pee Wee at Fairground (now Washington) and McDowell Avenues across from Washington School; the William Henry Harrison at Third and St. Clair Streets; and the Fort Sackville at Fifth and Vigo Streets. Further, that Fourth of July, John H. Chamberlain opened a miniature golf course at his Lincoln Trail Camp on State Road 61.

The Fort Sackville, being downtown, was not only one of the most patronized but also the most elaborate of the local courses. It opened to the public on June 22, 1930, but did not have its official opening until a week later, on the evening of June 28. The Fort Sackville was owned by local attorney Gilbert Alsop.

The course itself was colorful, with red, green and gold predominating. There were flower boxes, canopied tables and a gazing ball. The fence around the course even featured miniature replicas of Fort Sackville. There also was a dance pavilion, and patrons could enjoy the nearby Tal's Coffee Shop, run by Talmadge Woods.

The course had some challenging hazards and a practice fairway and green to the rear, where people were offered golfing instruction. It cost twenty-five cents to play the eighteen holes. Thirty-eight was considered par.

The ad for the formal opening read, in part, "Play miniature golf on this new course. Excellent playing conditions. Well lighted and extremely sporty. You'll enjoy it day or night. Healthful and the most fascinating game you ever played."

Mayor Joseph Kimmell had the honor of being the first person to tee off. Reverend Ray Montgomery, of the First Christian Church, made remarks. Women who played eighteen holes that evening were given roses, and the men received cigars. There was an orchestra and a quartet with free dancing.

Much competition existed between local players to see who could achieve the best score. On July 24, instructor Eddie Roellgen broke the course record at Fort Sackville when he shot a score of thirty-four. That bested the previous record of thirty-five held by Ray Beless. The women's record holder at the time was Clarice Kerr, a nurse at Good Samaritan Hospital, with a score of forty. All of the miniature golf courses had tournaments to help keep interest high. For instance, the Pee Wee had a tournament on July 26 with a first prize of five dollars for both the men's and women's winners.

Many other courses opened in Vincennes over the years. One of the most popular was Dinky Links on Niblack Boulevard, near Washington Avenue, just beyond Gregg Park. Dinky Links had its grand opening on July 7, 1945.

The miniature golf fad cooled, as all fads do, but miniature golf still remains an enjoyable type of recreation today.

49

NANCY GARDNER BAKER WAS LAST VINCENNES CIVIL WAR NURSE

On September 8, 1862, a Civil War troop train on the Ohio and Mississippi Railroad, carrying members of the Ninety-Eighth Illinois Infantry, was involved in a horrific accident near Bridgeport, Illinois. The wreck resulted when a switch was left open, causing the train to veer off the track and crash into a freight train. Eight men were killed and seventy-five more injured. Doctors from Vincennes and Lawrenceville went to the scene to give assistance. Many of the injured were cared for at St. Rose Academy in Vincennes (then at Second and Church Streets), which was transformed into a makeshift hospital.

Fast-forward some sixty-eight years after that tragedy. When readers of the *Vincennes Commercial* looked at their December 31, 1930 edition of the paper, they saw a brief front-page story headed "Woman Who Served as Nurse in Civil War Time Is Dead." This article announced the passing of Nancy Gardner Baker the previous day at the age of eighty-nine. In 1862, the then twenty-one-year-old Nancy Gardner had nursed some of the soldiers at St. Rose. She was reported to have been the last surviving Civil War nurse from this area.

Nancy Gardner was born in Vincennes on January 31, 1841, the daughter of Elbridge G. and Dorcas Fellows Gardner. Elbridge was the son of funeral home founder Andrew Gardner. Nancy married Hiram Baker on March 13, 1872. Hiram was employed as a carpenter.

Nancy Baker was one of three Vincennes women who nursed the men hurt in the accident. The others were Adeliah "Dee" Roseman, the sister of Joseph Roseman, who served in the war, and Katherine Wise (later Fay). None of the women had any medical training but pitched in as best they could.

Kate Fay died in Vincennes in 1886, and Dee Roseman passed away at her brother's home in Evansville in 1890. The remains of both woman rest in Vincennes's Greenlawn Cemetery.

Even later in life, Nancy Baker's devotion to country continued. During the United States' involvement in the First World War in 1917–18, a popular homefront activity for women was the knitting of socks and other garments to be sent overseas to servicemen. Baker was one of those who put her knitting needles to work, making sweaters and socks for the men.

She had family members who saw service in three wars: the Civil War, the Spanish-American War and the First World War.

Baker also helped establish the Knox County Orphanage and was a longtime orphanage board member.

Later in life, she was given honorary membership in the local Women's Relief Corps, an auxiliary of the Grand Army of the Republic, a fraternal organization for Union veterans. The group always honored her on Decoration Day (now Memorial Day). For instance, on Decoration Day 1928, bouquets of peonies were placed on Fay and Roseman's graves, and a similar bouquet was brought to Baker at her home. The American Legion Drum and Bugle Corps also serenaded her. Her birthday, too, was a big cause for celebration, with gifts, flowers and visits by friends.

Nancy Gardner Baker died at the family home at 519 North Seventh Street, where she was living with two nieces, Fannie and Alice Hall. She was just a month shy of her ninetieth birthday. Her husband preceded her in death. The local Spanish-American War veterans visited the residence as a group to pay their respects on New Year's Day 1931. The funeral was held from the home on January 2, with burial in Greenlawn Cemetery.

This is how the final lines of the editorial that was published in the New Year's Day edition of the *Commercial* praised Baker's service to country: "The courage and sacrifice that dictated that service in her youth characterized her throughout life. She lived bravely and she goes to the grave an honored soldier."

50
Daniel Hanes Was Symbol of a Bygone Era

When seventy-year-old Daniel Hanes died at his Vincennes home on the evening of March 7, 1932, it was the passing of a living link to a bygone era. By all accounts, Hanes was the last local man who had piloted steamboats on the Wabash River.

Steamboats on that stream were a common sight in the nineteenth century, transporting both goods and passengers. Dozens of boats plied the river, with grain and other agricultural products making up much of their cargo. The river was the principal means of transportation from pioneer days until the coming of the railroad.

Daniel Hanes was born in Illinois on May 15, 1861, to George and Hester Ellen Petrie Hanes. The family later moved to Vincennes. He married Rosa Alcorn on April 13, 1888, and the couple raised a large family.

Hanes first worked under Captain Allen Tindolph as a cabin boy, while the former was still in his teens. Tindolph was perhaps the best known of the local riverboat pilots. He began his career on the river in 1863, working himself up to captain and then boat owner. He had several different boats over the next quarter century, the most significant of which was the steamer *Crown Point*, often described as "the best boat ever built on the Wabash."

Like his one-time employer, Hanes advanced up the ladder to pilot a boat. His occupation in the 1883–84 edition of the Vincennes City Directory was fisherman. When the 1888–89 directory—the next extant edition—was published, Hanes was a steamboat pilot. The 1891–92 directory specifies that he was a pilot on the steamer *Russell*.

Hanes worked under Tindolph for some years, piloting the *Crown Point* between Vincennes and Terre Haute. He alternated piloting duties with Captain Felix Anderson. Tindolph ultimately sold the *Crown Point*, and it continued to operate on the Ohio River. Tindolph's career on the river ended in 1889 due to health reasons. He died in 1894.

Hanes piloted other boats as well. In early 1898, he went to Mount Carmel, Illinois, to take charge of the steamer *Irene*.

Steamboat pilots had to exercise great skill and have a thorough knowledge of the river. In May 1903, the *New Harmony Register* praised Hanes's ability, noting that from Vincennes to the mouth of the Wabash, he knew "every rock, snag, reef and bar" and could "tell you about the exact stage of the water over or around them any day in the year."

The passing of steamboats from the Wabash, the last of which were seen in the very beginning years of the twentieth century, was a gradual process and can be attributed to the filling up of the channel so that it was no longer navigable, especially when the water level was low. Further, more freight was being hauled on the cheaper, faster railroads and, later, by truck.

Following his steamboat days, Hanes settled down to life as a painting contractor, definitely a less exciting way of earning a living after so much time spent on the river. Despite decades of marriage and eight children, Daniel and Rosa Hanes eventually divorced. Rosa moved to Indianapolis, where she died in October 1931.

When Hanes died the following year at his Second and Scott Street home, he was survived by those eight children, all of whom divided his small estate. His funeral took place on March 9, with interment in Vincennes's Fairview Cemetery.

It was said that Hanes never lost hope that steamboats would someday return to the Wabash. One can almost imagine him, in his later years, gazing out over the river and dwelling fondly on a time long past.

51
KNOX COUNTY GIRL NAMED CHAMPION IN INTERNATIONAL CANNING CONTEST

In 1932, a seventeen-year-old Knox County girl named Dorothea Buckthal gained national and even international recognition for her family and community as a result of her home economics skills. Dorothea's story is a bittersweet one, as her honor came to her posthumously.

Dorothea Buckthal was born on November 14, 1915, and lived on a farm near Freelandville with her parents, Paul and Anna, and two brothers, Elmer and Walter. She was a member of the Bethel Evangelical Church, having been confirmed there in 1926.

Dorothea was active in 4-H and won many awards in both local and state fair competitions. She especially excelled at canning the produce grown on her family's farm. Dorothea graduated from Freelandville High School in the spring of 1932 and hoped to attend Butler University that fall.

Dorothea did not feel well that summer after graduation. On August 24, her parents took her to a doctor in Bicknell who removed her tonsils and adenoids. Later that day, she began hemorrhaging and had to be transported to Good Samaritan Hospital. Even though specialists attended her, the hemorrhaging could not be stopped, and she died in the wee hours of the following morning. It was then determined that she was a hemophiliac.

Her funeral was held on August 27, with burial in Bethel Church Cemetery.

Prior to her untimely death, Dorothea had planned to enter some of her canned goods in the International Canning Contest held at Aurora, Illinois, a suburb of Chicago. Her mother decided to send in her entry: six jars of food that made up a balanced meal. The six jars contained corn and tomato soup, beef cubes, string beans, apple butter, pickle relish and blackberries. All of the food, including the beef, was raised on the Buckthal farm.

On October 21, Anna Buckthal received notification that her daughter's entry had won grand champion, beating thousands of entries sent in from all over the world, it was said, some fifty thousand entries.

For having the winning entry, Paul and Anna, along with their son Walter (Elmer was then a student at Indiana University), went to Chicago courtesy of Marshall Field's Department Store, where Anna received Dorothea's prizes, including one hundred dollars, a silver loving cup, all kinds of kitchen utensils and equipment and even a complete clothing ensemble. A special banquet for the winner was held in the store's famous tearoom.

On November 2, Anna was heard on the radio program the *National Farm and Home Hour*, and people back home listened to the broadcast. She talked about the importance of canning as a money-saver and noted that she currently had around three hundred cans in her cellar. The story was also written up in the farm publication *Breeders' Gazette* and a number of newspapers.

In 1966, to commemorate the Freelandville Centennial, a history was published that included a short item about the canning championship. The item noted that thirty-four years after the event, Dorothea's mother still had four of the cans that had been entered in the contest, all of which were sealed with glass lids.

52
Vincennes Mayoral Election of 1934 Was a Nail-Biter

After the mayoral election of November 6, 1934, the following day's edition of the *Vincennes Sun-Commercial* carried this bold headline: "Republican Mayor, Democratic Council Is Elected by Vincennes." The paper was touting the slim election victory of Republican challenger F. Albert Reiman over incumbent Democratic mayor Joseph Kimmell. Only fifteen votes separated the two candidates.

The *Vincennes Post*'s headline of November 8 was a little more restrained. It read, "Apparent Totals Elect Reiman by 15."

As the votes were counted that election eve, Kimmell had a lead that seemed as if it could not be overcome, but when the count was complete, Reiman, a longtime local florist and building and loan official, had won by that slim fifteen-vote margin. The final tabulation was 4,601 votes for Reiman and 4,586 votes for Kimmell.

It was the closest mayoral election in Vincennes history.

On November 10, Kimmell filed a petition before Judge William S. Hoover in the Knox Circuit Court for a recount of votes, citing errors in the count. On November 15, Curtis Shake, William M. Willmore and Allen E. Hogue were appointed recount commissioners. Shake was the Democrat's choice, Willmore was selected by Reiman and Hogue was chosen by the court. At 8:00 a.m. on Monday, November 19, the official recount began at the Knox County Courthouse.

When it was complete the following morning, the tide had turned, and Kimmell, with a lead of just seven votes, was declared the winner, albeit by an even slimmer margin than that which had led him to contest Reiman's victory. It was really just the start of the legal wrangling.

On November 20, acting on a petition filed by Reiman's attorneys, Hoover issued a temporary injunction to stop the certification of Kimmell's election, but the election was certified and Kimmell took the oath before the clerk had knowledge of the order. They also petitioned to dismiss the recount board. Hoover sustained the objection of Kimmell's attorneys regarding the latter point. Knox County Superior Court judge William F. Calverley heard the case over the injunction, and the injunction was dissolved on November 26.

Joseph Kimmell, who was twice elected mayor of Vincennes by narrow margins. *Knox County Public Library's McGrady-Brockman House.*

On November 29, Kimmell was quoted as saying: "I have been declared elected by a regularly constituted Board of Recount. I have qualified as the next mayor of Vincennes. I intend to stick. Never in my life have I run from a fight that I thought was right. I know that I am right in this matter and I won't retreat an inch unless compelled to do so by the courts."

Kimmell began his second term at noon on January 1, 1935. Reiman even showed up at city hall that day demanding the office, but he was turned away. Although the encounter was a civil one, Reiman was far from finished in his efforts to wrest the office from Kimmell.

The next step in what became a complex battle fought in the courtroom took place on January 3, when Reiman filed an action of mandamus in the Knox Circuit Court to force Kimmell to turn over the office. A demurrer was then filed on behalf of Kimmell. The demurrer was sustained by special judge Sullivan attorney Charles Hunt on February 11.

The legal back and forth continued not for months, but for years, as Kimmell carried out the duties of his office. Reiman took his fight all the way to the state supreme court, which on November 9, 1937, three years after the election, ruled that Reiman "has not shown that he has a clear legal right to the immediate possession of the office."

Joe Kimmell was no stranger to close elections. When he was elected mayor in 1929, he defeated his Republican opponent, Perry Green, by just twenty-four votes. A recount was also held that year, with Kimmell adding fifteen votes to his lead.

53

SALLY RAND BROUGHT HER RISQUÉ SHOW TO THE PANTHEON THEATER IN 1935

In the 1930s, Sally Rand became one of the most famous and controversial performers of her day. Rand popularized both the fan dance and the bubble dance, and in both she gave the illusion that she was completely nude. While these performances would be considered G-rated in our more permissive times, they were viewed by many in that era as obscene.

Sally Rand was born Helen Gould Beck in Missouri in 1904. She began her career in vaudeville and then was an acrobatic dancer, even traveling with a circus. She later appeared in silent films. It was claimed that director Cecil B. DeMille gave her the name Sally Rand, taken from a *Rand McNally Atlas*.

It would be in burlesque that Sally Rand made her mark. She first gained fame at the 1933 Chicago World's Fair, also called the Century of Progress International Exposition, where she introduced her fan dance. She danced with big ostrich feather fans to the music of Claude Debussy's "Clair de Lune" and Chopin's "Waltz in C sharp minor." The scandalous act created a sensation and led to Rand being arrested numerous times.

She later did a similar dance using a five-foot balloon, which eliminated the problem of the feathers blowing if her shows were outdoors.

Rand performs her fan dance in the 1934 film *Bolero*, starring George Raft and Carole Lombard. That movie came out in pre-Code Hollywood. Later that same year, censorship guidelines began to be enforced, governing what could be seen on screen.

Sally Rand came to Vincennes on Saturday, June 8, 1935, while on a tour of the Midwest, performing a single midnight show on stage at the

Left: Risqué performer Sally Rand posing in 1937. *Library of Congress Prints and Photographs Division, Washington D.C.*

Below: Downtown Vincennes with a view of the Pantheon Theater, where Sally Rand and many other famous entertainers took the stage. *Norbert Brown Collection.*

Pantheon Theater. (The curtain rose at 11:30 p.m.). She brought with her a large troupe of performers, thirty in all, including Marguerite Ware, who did musical comedy; William and Joe Mandel, comedy headliners; and a group of female dancers. Prior to her tour, she had been performing at the Paradise Club in New York City.

Large ads in the *Vincennes Sun-Commercial* boasted: "The one and only Sally Rand in Person on the Stage in her New and Beautiful Bubble Dance and World Famous Fan Dance." The ads themselves were even a bit risqué for the time.

All seats were reserved and cost seventy-five cents for the lower floor and mezzanine and fifty-five cents for the family circle and balcony.

Although Sally Rand's appearance was touted as "the big theater event of the season," and seat sales were good, tickets were still available on the day of the show. In promoting the performance, the theater's management also addressed its controversial nature, stating in the *Sun-Commercial*, "Although Miss Rand has been criticized for her fan dance, most of those who heaped this criticism upon her have never seen her do the dance they denounce."

There is no record of how many people actually attended the Vincennes show, but no doubt Rand's dances were witnessed by a large and appreciative audience.

Sally Rand continued to perform even late in her life. She died in California, at the age of seventy-five, on August 31, 1979. Burial was in Oakland Memorial Park Cemetery in Glendora, California.

54

THE 1936 HEAT WAVE WAS THE WORST IN HISTORY, PART 1

The summer of 1936 remains one of the hottest ever experienced in North America. Numerous record-high temperatures were set that year, records that remain unbroken even today. The heat caused untold suffering and led to as many as five thousand deaths in the United States and many more in Canada. The heat wave covered virtually the entire country, with the Upper Midwest and the Plains states the most severely affected.

The fact that the nation was in the midst of the Great Depression, with millions of people experiencing economic hardship, only added to the misery. The oppressive hot weather was accompanied by drought in many states, most notably the Plains, where Dust Bowl conditions drove families from their homes.

The record heat began in late June and lasted through the month of July. At Vincennes, during the first two weeks of June 1936, all attention was focused on the June 14 dedication of the George Rogers Clark Memorial, one of the biggest days in the city's history. While it was hot for the dedication, conditions were nothing like what Mother Nature was to dole out in the coming days.

On June 17, the temperature at Vincennes reached 102 degrees, and the official start of summer was still a few days away. With the heat came dry conditions, although this aided farmers in harvesting wheat and putting up clover hay. A light rain fell on the night of June 21–22, benefitting the corn crop and bringing some temporary relief. By the end of the month, the heat had returned, and crops were being affected by the lack of rain.

The thermometer at Vincennes pushed up to 106 degrees on June 29. In total, there would be nineteen days that June when the local temperature surpassed 90 degrees.

The mercury continued to climb through the first days of July. It was 98 degrees at Vincennes on Saturday, July 4, 104 degrees on July 5 and a sweltering 107 degrees on July 6. All of those official temperature readings were taken by A.B. Brouillette, the local weather observer for the U.S. Weather Bureau.

Of course, these were the days before air conditioning was widely available. In 1935, the Pantheon Theater became the first Vincennes business to install air conditioning, with others to gradually follow. Air conditioning was unknown in private homes at this time, so, overall, residents had to cope the best they could. Many people slept outdoors, either on their porches or in their yards to get some relief. Any body of water, be it a pond, lake or creek, became a popular place to cool off. Rainbow Beach Pool didn't exist then. It wouldn't open until 1937.

Vincennes got just over an inch of rain on July 6, the day the temperature had hit 107 degrees, and there were isolated showers at other points in the county. Oaktown got its first rain in several weeks on July 8, aiding the melon crop. That afternoon, Vincennes and vicinity were hit by what was described as a "baby tornado." Trees were uprooted, and homes and garages had their roofs damaged. Orchardists got the worst of the storm, as dozens of apple trees were downed; twenty fell at the orchard of Vincennes mayor Joseph Kimmell. Will Teschner lost fifty apple trees. Bushels of early apples were also blown from trees.

Even after the storm, there was little respite from the heat. On July 9, it was 103 degrees, and the temperature reached 107 on July 10.

One irony of the summer heat wave was that Vincennes had faced a bitter cold winter, with many days of subzero temperatures (it was actually seventeen degrees below zero at Vincennes on January 27). This led the *Vincennes Sun-Commercial*, in its Friday, July 10 edition, to colorfully comment, "Old Man Mercury who went way down in the cellar last January and February and killed all the peaches, continued in the villain role Friday, going up in the attic with vicious designs on the corn and cantaloupes, and all the other crops."

Vincennes and Knox County remained in the grip of the heat wave for the remainder of July, with the worst conditions yet to come.

55
ALL-TIME RECORD HIGH TEMPERATURE REACHED LOCALLY, PART 2

In July 1936, the United States remained in the grip of the worst heat wave the country had ever known, with day after day of temperatures in the triple digits. The nationwide death toll from the weather was rising, and there would be several heat-related deaths in and around Knox County.

The official temperature readings at Vincennes continued to climb. On July 10, it edged up to 107 degrees and on July 11, 106 degrees was recorded. Every part of Indiana was above the century mark.

On July 13, the all-time record high of 110 degrees in the city that had been set on July 30, 1930, was tied, and on Tuesday, July 14, Vincennes set a new record, with the *Vincennes Sun-Commercial* declaring, "Hottest Day in Local History Recorded Here." At 2:30 that afternoon, the official government thermometer rose to a blistering 111 degrees. Records fell in cities throughout the state. The following day, Vincennes hit 108 degrees, and all that kept the thermometer from going higher were rain clouds that rolled in, obscuring the sun.

The Vincennes Fire Department helped cool off the city's children by taking one of its trucks out to various intersections, where firefighters roped off the streets and opened the hose nozzle. Hundreds of children frolicked in the water. They were described as a "carefree mob, shouting with glee."

Naturally, the weather was the chief topic of conversation, although one local doctor offered same sage advice: "Quit talking about how hot it is. Keep your mind off it. Why only a few months ago, when everything was snow and ice and the thermometer was sub-zero, think of the people who said they never would complain again about the heat."

The unbearable conditions proved fatal to some. On July 10, forty-three-year-old George Halter was discovered dead in his bed at a North Tenth Street boardinghouse. Halter's death was attributed, in part, to the heat. On July 15, a Decker Township man, sixty-eight-year-old Smith Lansdown, died when he was overcome after picking cantaloupes. That same day, a St. Francisville man died of heat prostration. On July 16, eighty-year-old Mary Alice Moore of Vincennes died of heat stroke.

The heat was so intense that streets suffered what were termed "blow-ups"—the pavement actually swelled and burst. There were as many as fifteen incidents of this happening all over Vincennes, forcing street department employees to do repairs out in the sweltering weather.

On July 18, the high at Vincennes was 92 degrees, and that was the lowest high in more than two weeks. The worst of the heat was over, although drought still prevailed in many areas. On July 25, Vincennes had just over an inch of rain. Decker recorded 1.75 inches, providing a big boost to the cantaloupe, watermelon and tomato crops.

While the heat wave was broken, there would still be some hot days that summer. On July 26, 100 degrees was recorded at Vincennes and 103 was hit on July 27. In August, there were several days when the temperature went above 100 degrees.

In total, there were fourteen days that July when the temperature at Vincennes exceeded the 100-degree mark. For the entire month, there were only seven days when the high temperature was under 90 degrees. The lowest daily high that month was 81 degrees.

Turtle Derby Was an Amusing Civic Undertaking

In the spring of 1936, a Junior Chamber of Commerce, later known as the Jaycees, was organized at Vincennes for young business and professional men. The junior chamber was modeled after a similar organization at Evansville. The group undertook projects for civic betterment.

One community fundraiser the junior chamber sponsored that same year was the Turtle Derby, held on the afternoon of Sunday, September 20 at Washington Field.

The premise of the Turtle Derby was simple. Both businesses and individuals paid five dollars to sponsor a turtle in a race, with the winners awarded cash prizes. The turtles were turned loose inside an enclosed seventy-five-foot-wide circle. The enclosure was then removed and the first turtle to reach the edge of the circle was the winner. There were six heats, with one-, two- and three-dollar prizes for the top three places in each heat, and grand prizes of ten, twenty and thirty dollars. Small attendance prizes were awarded between heats.

As the *Vincennes Sun-Commercial* stated, "The turtles will race for cash and glory. The cash prizes will go to the sponsors and the glory to the turtles."

The turtles were on loan from the Evansville Junior Chamber, which staged its own Turtle Derby at Bosse Field. The reptiles were small in size, just four to six inches long, and came from a place called Turtle Cove near New Harmony. The shell of each turtle was painted and had a small flag attached. The turtles were not fed for a couple of days before the race so they would be especially active when released.

The names of all the entrants were posted on a sign in front of city hall. Also on display there, as a means of promoting the derby, was an approximately three-foot-long leatherback turtle, on loan from the Indiana Department of Conservation.

Marvin Critchfield was general chairman of the event, and his committee chairs were David Fox, Wallace Howe and Joe Riley.

Response to the derby was overwhelming, with some 113 entries. Judges for the races were Dexter Gardner, president of the Vincennes Chamber of Commerce; Vincennes University president Walter A. Davis; Ernest Owens, secretary of the Evansville Junior Chamber of Commerce; and Joe V. Riley, vice-president of the local junior chamber. Mayor Joseph Kimmell was the official starter for the 2:00 p.m. event. Admission was ten cents.

All of the turtles were given fanciful names that reflected something about their sponsors. The thirty-dollar grand-prize winner was a turtle named H.C. Special whose sponsor was Vincennes resident Bob Morgan. The Gimbel-Bond Company's entry, named Vincennes' Greatest Store, was second, and Knox County sheriff Clarence "Gus" Joice's Sheriff Special placed third.

The fastest time that day was two minutes and fifty-two seconds, and the slowest was four minutes, thirty-three seconds.

The proceeds from the 1936 derby were used by the junior chamber to place a large sign on U.S. 41 South, advertising the city's tourist sites.

The Turtle Derby would be a popular annual event in Vincennes for several more years.

57
VINCENNES TOOK IN EVANSVILLE FLOOD REFUGEES IN 1937

In the wee hours of Thursday morning, January 28, 1937, six buses rolled into Vincennes carrying 160 refugees from Evansville, who had been driven from their homes by the record-breaking Ohio River flood. Of that group, there were approximately fifty-five men and twenty children (including a three-week-old baby), and the remainder were women. All were African Americans.

The devastation in Evansville was immense, with major flooding throughout the city. Flood stage for the Ohio at that point was 35.0 feet, and the river crested at 53.8 feet. Martial law had been declared there.

The buses, which were not heated, were over nine hours late in arriving, and local officials became anxious due to the delay. It turned out that not only had one bus broken down, but the drivers also lost their way, having been forced by floodwaters to take a longer, alternate route.

The cold, tired and hungry group was first taken to the Union Depot Hotel, which stood near the intersection of Wabash and Washington Avenues. There they were served a meal of mulligan stew, bread and butter and hot coffee. All of the refugees then had to be registered in case other family members tried to locate them.

The men and the older boys were then housed at the Squibb Distillery building on East Indianapolis Avenue and the women at two churches: the Second Baptist Church at Twelfth and Seminary Streets and the Bethel African Methodist Episcopal Church at Tenth and Buntin Streets.

These housing arrangements were quickly deemed inadequate, as the buildings were cold and crowded, and there was little for the visitors to do. That afternoon, the women and children were relocated to the Union Depot Hotel. The men were moved the next morning. The entire group was being transported to the hotel for meals anyway. The building was empty and on the verge of being razed. The flood refugees would be the final "guests" to stay there.

A few of the displaced were sick from their ordeal, so a temporary hospital was set up at the hotel, staffed by nurses from Good Samaritan Hospital, under the supervision of hospital superintendent Edith Willis. Only one person, who was suffering from pneumonia, was transported to Good Samaritan.

Overall, it was a well-organized effort on the part of Vincennes, with various committees, such as food and registration, established to make every part of the group's stay run smoothly. The local Red Cross supplied everyone with shoes and warm clothing.

They were given two meals a day: breakfast, followed by dinner at 4:00 p.m. Dinner on Friday was spareribs and sauerkraut, baked beans, boiled potatoes, canned tomatoes, bread pudding and milk and coffee.

Besides food, clothing and medical care, it was important to provide entertainment. A request went out to the community for toys and games,

The Union Depot Hotel, where Evansville flood refugees were housed in 1937. The building was razed later that same year. *Knox County Public Library's McGrady-Brockman House.*

and the children were read stories. For the adult women, there were sewing classes. The men played checkers, and a call was put out for radios. Church services were held on Sunday, and roast chicken and dumplings was on the dinner menu that day.

They were all so happy to be in a safe and warm environment that they gladly pitched in with chores, cleaning, scrubbing floors and washing dishes. The refugees stayed in Vincennes for nearly two weeks. The group left for Evansville by train on February 8 in much better condition than when they came. Drinks and sandwiches were sent with them.

The Bethel Evangelical Church at Freelandville had housed nineteen Evansville flood victims, and they returned home on February 7.

The rooms of the Union Depot Hotel, which had so much life breathed into them for those few days, were then vacant for good, and the old landmark was torn down in August of that year.

58
William Strange Was One of the Last Knox County Civil War Veterans

William Albert Strange was born in Loogootee on June 13, 1850, and was destined to live an uneventful life in that small Midwest town before the Civil War and his own adventurous spirit intervened. Strange was one of the youngest men to enlist in the war (he claimed to be the youngest) and followed his service with several years living and working in the American West.

William Strange's parents, Charles and Rebecca Bramble Strange, were both natives of Kentucky, and as a boy, their son was apprenticed to a jeweler, work that he found tedious.

The story goes that William's brother came home from the war on leave and recounted his experiences, exciting to the boy and motivating him to leave his dull apprenticeship and attempt to enlist, even though he was underage.

In early 1864, the thirteen-year-old Strange was in Centralia, Illinois, where the 143rd Illinois Infantry had its camp. Almost as a lark, the boy was placed on guard duty at a gate and told that no one could get through without signed orders. When an Irishman who was inebriated tried to pass, Strange clubbed the man over the head, knocking him out. Impressed by this bravado, a captain who saw the tearful boy watching the soldiers depart let him board the train. He was mustered in under the false age of eighteen in Company E of the 143rd on June 1, 1864, under Colonel Dudley C. Smith. The boy was equipped with a Springfield rifle and ended up on picket duty in Memphis, Tennessee. He even found himself under fire.

At war's end, Strange's desire for adventure continued, and he traveled to the West. There, he held many colorful jobs, including wagon train driver, sheep herder, Indian fighter, Wild West Show entertainer, policeman and mail rider. He also had the opportunity to meet some of the major western personalities of that era, among them Buffalo Bill, Wild Bill Hickok and Calamity Jane.

In 1880, he married Julia Jackson in Missouri. Julia died there, and Strange eventually settled in Knox County. He was a stone mason by occupation.

William Albert Strange died at his son's home in Bruceville on February 25, 1938. He was eighty-seven years old. Five children survived him: Mary Fenton of Oklahoma, Cora Parker of Washington, Clara Brown of Colorado, Anna Martin of Kansas and William A. Jr. of Bruceville. A sixth child had died in infancy. There were twenty-seven grandchildren and ten great-grandchildren.

The funeral was held at the Bruceville Methodist Church on February 27, with burial in Vincennes's Fairview Cemetery.

At the time of his death, Strange was one of only a handful of surviving Civil War veterans living in Knox County. When the year 1938 began, there were six veterans of the Civil War in the county. Along with Strange, four others died that year. These were Charles Dixon, who died in Vincennes at the age of ninety-eight on January 22; Henry Burns, who died at Sandborn at age eighty-nine on March 10; Ezekiel Beard, who died at Monroe City at age ninety-four on May 18; and William Wyant, who died in Harrison Township on June 3 at the age of ninety-seven.

The last local veteran of the Civil War, Alexander Bowen, died in Vincennes at the age of ninety-eight on December 31, 1941.

59
DUKE ELLINGTON TOOK THE STAGE AT VINCENNES

On Sunday, December 17, 1939, one of the premier entertainers of the twentieth century appeared at the Pantheon Theater in Vincennes. It was on that day that jazz great Duke Ellington and his orchestra took the stage for a series of shows.

By 1939, Duke Ellington had already achieved fame as a jazz musician. He was a pianist and a big band leader and was perhaps best known for composing the music of classic songs such as "Mood Indigo," "It Don't Mean a Thing (If It Ain't Got That Swing") and "Sophisticated Lady." He and his orchestra were popular performers at Harlem's Cotton Club and toured extensively through the 1930s.

The Pantheon gave Ellington's appearance heavy promotion, billing him as "Harlem's Aristocrat of Jazz!" and boasting that the show featured "The Largest and Most Expensive Traveling Orchestra That We Have Ever Offered at Popular Prices." Admission, depending on seating, ranged from fifteen to forty cents.

The day of the Ellington show, a Pantheon ad announced: "One of the most outstanding entertainment programs ever offered in any theater big or small is lined up for a continuous showing today only at the Pantheon."

It was perhaps no coincidence that such a noteworthy act was booked at the Pantheon that December, since that same month, on December 14, a competitor, Theodore Charles, had the grand opening of his New Moon Theater just down the street on the corner of Sixth and Main.

Duke Ellington performing in New York City in May 1943. Ellington appeared at Vincennes's Pantheon Theater in 1939. *Library of Congress, Prints and Photographs Division, Washington, D.C.*

Also taking the stage with Ellington and his band was Ivie Anderson, a popular singer who was part of Ellington's show from 1931 until her retirement in 1942.

There was a feature picture on the bill that day, a comedy called *Joe and Ethel Turp Call on the President*, which stars Ann Sothern.

There is little on the written record about Duke Ellington's actual Vincennes shows. Local papers did no follow-up on his appearance, gave no attendance figures and no description of the performance. There were a few lines of published recollections of local people decades later, indicating that the shows were well-attended. It certainly had to be an unforgettable entertainment experience for all of those fortunate enough to be present.

As for Duke Ellington, his career would span several more decades and he would receive countless honors, including a total of thirteen Grammy Awards, the Presidential Medal of Freedom and a posthumous Pulitzer Prize. He died in 1974 at the age of seventy-five.

PART V
1940–1950

60

Main and Busseron Streets Became One-Way

Traffic flow on two major streets in downtown Vincennes underwent a major change in January 1940. It was that month when both Main and Busseron Streets, which had up to that time been two-way, were designated one-way streets, Main between Second and Sixth Streets and Busseron from Sixth to First Streets.

Mayor Albert B. Taylor, along with local businessmen, made the announcement on November 7, 1939. The reason for the change was to help alleviate the severe traffic congestion on those two streets. At the time, Main was being resurfaced, so it was thought that the change would take effect in a couple of weeks, but in early December, the mayor stated that it would be postponed until after the holidays so as to avoid confusion downtown during the busy shopping season.

The change was begun on a trial basis on January 3, 1940. Main Street traffic traveled west to east (the opposite direction that it does today), and Busseron traffic went west in the direction of the river.

Not all downtown businesspeople were necessarily on board with the new traffic pattern. As the *Vincennes Sun-Commercial* reported in the January 1 edition, "Merchants generally have expressed a resigned attitude to the new traffic restrictions, showing a willingness to try out the new one-way traffic regulations to see how the motoring public adopts it before voicing any protest."

Of course, Vincennes Transit Inc. had to make some changes in bus routes (buses replaced streetcars in 1938) and even published a newspaper

This photo of Vincennes's Main Street from the 1930s shows busy two-way traffic. Traffic was made one-way in 1948. *Knox County Public Library's McGrady-Brockman House.*

ad on January 2, with the aim of increasing business. The ad read: "Avoid the Confusion of One-Way Traffic! Ride the Bus."

The majority of motorists did fine with the new traffic flow—although, as might be expected, a few were caught going the wrong way. The change did not affect parking regulations on Main Street. Thirty-minute parking remained the rule, with a two-dollar fine for the first violation. There was no time limit on Busseron.

The city's initial experiment with one-way traffic on these downtown streets was short-lived. On March 11, a little over two months after the change started, the Vincennes City Council voted unanimously to return to two-way streets. A survey of business owners on Main Street revealed that a majority wanted to go back. A number of them spoke at the meeting either before or against one-way streets. William Duesterberg commented that he felt it was confusing to people who came into Vincennes from out of town. Ed O'Neil, superintendent of Vincennes Transit Inc., while not offering an opinion, did state that he felt the establishment of one-way streets had dramatically increased incidents of double parking, which was problematic for the bus drivers.

Tinkering with traffic flow on Main and Busseron Streets was not at an end. A few years later, in January 1947, a Purdue University Public Safety Institute Report that had been prepared some months earlier was presented to the Vincennes City Council, the City Plan Commission and the Chamber of Commerce Traffic Safety Committee. One of the report's major recommendations was that both Main and Busseron Streets be made one-way, with the direction reversed from what had previously been instituted, so as to better reflect the natural flow of traffic.

It was stated that, ideally, both streets should be two-way, with parking prohibited, but this was not possible due to limited parking downtown.

On April 16, 1948, Mayor William Betz announced that in the business section, Main and Busseron Streets would again be made one-way, with traffic flow in the direction suggested in the report. The change began on April 22, with few problems encountered.

Of course, Main Street remains one-way today. Busseron Street was made two-way in 2002, when the Vincennes Police Department relocated to the former post office building at 501 Busseron Street.

Knox County Townships Plagued by Mosquitoes

The spring of 1940 found residents of Decker Township and Lower Vincennes Township suffering through the worst infestation of mosquitoes that anyone living in that part of Knox County could remember. Swarms of the biting insects made spending any amount of time outdoors intolerable. Conditions were so bad that it was almost impossible for farmers to use horses and mules to work their fields. Farmers on tractors had to have smudge pots with them to ward off the pests.

Decker Township possessed ideal conditions for the insects to breed. The township was bordered by both the White and Wabash Rivers and contained large ponds, such as Claypole and Long Pond. Further, eight hundred acres of the once vast Cypress Swamp remained, where mosquitoes could thrive.

Not only were the mosquitoes a great annoyance, but there also were fears that some might carry malaria.

On May 29, with the situation worsening, a meeting of the two townships' farmers was held at the Decker Chapel High School. Around 150 men turned out to discuss the problem.

The accepted way of dealing with mosquitoes in those days was to pour motor oil into the bodies of water in order to kill the newly hatched larvae. This is what would be undertaken in Decker and Vincennes Townships that spring.

At the meeting of farmers, a five-man advisory group was formed, with each man in charge of showing where the worst breeding places for the mosquitoes were in specific parts of the townships. These five men were Charles Thompson, Ralph Johnson, Ed Steckler, Elmer Doades and Tony Smith.

1940–1950

Cypress Swamp down in Knox County's "Neck" was one of the places that battled swarms of mosquitoes in the spring of 1940. *Knox County Public Library's McGrady-Brockman House.*

Young men who were part of the Civilian Conservation Corps in Washington, Indiana, were to be brought to Knox County and undertook the actual work of pouring the oil. They would be under the supervision of CCC camp engineer Lawrence Bassett.

On May 31, the following men toured the affected parts of the townships: assistant county agricultural agent Lowell G. Taylor, Lawrence Bassett, Decker Township farmer Charles Thompson, CCC camp agronomist E.H. Ashworth and a reporter with the *Vincennes Sun-Commercial.*

On June 2, Knox County agricultural agent Henry S. Benson put out a call for filling stations and others to donate their old oil to be used in the battle. Benson estimated that a minimum of two thousand gallons of oil would be required, half that amount for Cypress Swamp alone. By June 5, one thousand gallons had been collected. Some responding to the call for oil were auto dealers Bruce C. Kixmiller and Elson G. Sims, along with Allegra Brothers Standard Service Station and Lane's Diamond Service Station.

The oil was spread in several different ways. Sometimes a boat with an oil drum was taken out and the oil poured over the side through a small hole in the drum. In small bodies of water, a quart can of oil with a hole in it was tossed in the water and the oil allowed to slowly seep out. Oil was even sprayed directly onto brush growing around water.

People were asked to aid in the effort by dumping any containers of standing water. Horse troughs were to be cleaned regularly.

By June 9, the CCC boys had already used over six hundred gallons of oil, and on June 11 they were scheduled to start their work in Cypress Swamp.

The spreading of oil, although harmful to the environment, was effective in helping eradicate the mosquitoes. Another thing that aided the effort, although obviously not beneficial to crops, was a dry spell that lingered until mid-July.

Vincennes High School Graduates of 1882 Recognized

On the evening of Friday, June 16, 1882, eleven Vincennes High School seniors took the stage at what was then known as Green's Opera House for the school's ninth annual commencement exercises.

Those eleven students were Carrie Houser, John Bierhaus, Ella Davidson, Justus Chancellor, Gertie Dodge, Eustach Companiott, Libbie Downes, Anna Gibson, George A. Miller, Rosa Root and John H. Niblack. Niblack had the honor of being valedictorian, and Houser was salutatorian. The class motto was *Gradatim*, which meant "by degrees" or "gradually" in Latin.

At that time, the high school was on the north side of Buntin Street, between Sixth and Seventh Streets. The board of school trustees was made up of Thomas Borrowman, Richard J. McKenney and John N. Convery. The school superintendent was R.A. Townsend.

In those days, each graduate stood and made an oration during the ceremony. The titles of some of that year's speeches, which give some idea of the general themes, were "Leave Behind a Shining Path," "Preparation," "One Learns by Failing" and "Usefulness the True Test of Merit." In between the speeches were various musical numbers.

Following the 1882 commencement, Vincennes High School had 117 alumni.

Fast-forward to the mid-twentieth century: in 1942, the 1882 class marked its sixtieth anniversary, and the surviving members were honored at the May 25 commencement ceremony. Six members of that class were still living, and five of them were able to attend. Those five were John Bierhaus and Anna Gibson Bierhaus (the classmates married on November 22, 1888,

Right: Ella Davidson, who served as head of the Vincennes Public Library from 1913 to 1925, was part of the Vincennes High School class of 1882. *Knox County Public Library's McGrady-Brockman House.*

Below: The Grand Opera House at Second and Busseron Streets, where the Vincennes High School commencement was held for many years. *Knox County Public Library's McGrady-Brockman House.*

and of course, John was known for his wholesale grocery business); Justus Chancellor, then an attorney in Chicago; John Niblack, former Wheatland store owner, then living in Waveland, Indiana; and Ella Davidson, who resided in Evansville. Davidson was head librarian of the Vincennes Public Library from 1913 to 1925. She had also been a librarian at Bloomington. Gertie Dodge Harris, of Kalamazoo, Michigan, was unable to be present.

Margaret Holland, a graduate of the class of 1874 and the only member of the 1882 faculty who was still living, was invited to the event, but she was unable to attend due to illness.

In 1942, commencement was held at the Vincennes Coliseum (not yet named Adams Coliseum). Of course, the school was then known as Lincoln High School, having been given that name in 1916, and was located on the north side of Buntin Street between Fifth and Sixth Streets. There were 229 graduates that year, the second-largest class up to that time, and the first since U.S. entry into the Second World War. John Bierhaus toasted the new class from the "old-timers," and principal and acting superintendent L.V. Phillips handed the five alumni special certificates.

Only a few years after the 1942 commencement, John Niblack passed away. Niblack died at Lapel, Indiana, on March 13, 1948. Justus Chancellor died in California on December 6, 1953. Ella Davidson and John Bierhaus both died in 1956, Davidson in Evansville on August 7 and Bierhaus at his Vincennes home on November 25. Anna Bierhaus passed away at Good Samaritan Hospital, at the age of ninety-four, on April 8, 1959.

63
ABBOTT AND COSTELLO WAR BOND DAY

At noon on Friday, August 14, 1942, a special joint meeting and luncheon of the Vincennes Rotary and Vincennes Kiwanis Clubs was held at the Jewel Café at 29 North Third Street. Also present were city officials, U.S. Army officials and members of the local war bond staff. The assembled crowd was awaiting the arrival of two prominent guests. Due at the café at that hour was the popular comedy team of Bud Abbott and Lou Costello, who were conducting war bond rallies all across the country. Newspaper publisher Eugene C. Pulliam (then publisher of the *Vincennes Sun-Commercial*), who was war bond chairman for Indiana, arranged for the pair to come to Vincennes.

During the Second World War, Hollywood stars aided the war effort in numerous ways, including joining the military, performing for the troops, appearing in war movies and promoting the sale of war savings bonds and stamps. Greer Garson, Bette Davis and Rita Hayworth were just a few of the entertainers who traveled the country to aid in selling war bonds.

Abbott and Costello had achieved fame on the stage, in radio and in the movies (and later television), exhibiting flawless timing and incredible chemistry. Their careers took off in 1941 with the popular film *Buck Privates*, and they made movies throughout the 1940s and '50s, among them the 1948 classic *Abbott and Costello Meet Frankenstein*. In conjunction with their Vincennes visit, their movie *Pardon My Sarong* opened at the Fort Sackville Theater on Main Street.

The comedians were on a grueling eighty-city tour that had started three weeks earlier, during which they paid all of their own expenses. They had come from Indianapolis, and were scheduled to be in Evansville at 3:00 p.m., so there wasn't time for them to give a big public program. The Jewel Café seated only 140 people, so attendance was very limited. They were running late for their Vincennes appearance and kept their audience waiting for over an hour.

Indiana congressman Gerald Landis spoke to the Rotary and Kiwanis before their guests arrived. Former mayor Joseph Kimmell officiated at the luncheon. L.V. Phillips, Knox County war bond chairman, also was present.

From the minute Abbott and Costello got to the café, the pair kept up a nonstop banter. Some children had come to see them, and there was even a crying baby, which they called "the youngest heckler that they had encountered." It was noted that Costello downed several glasses of iced tea.

Their brief show began at about 1:30 p.m. and was carried over WAOV Radio. Abbott and Costello delighted the crowd by performing their most famous routine, *Who's on First?* Afterward, they autographed some war bonds.

The two were accompanied to Vincennes by the following individuals: Tom McCloud, their manager; W.B. Stevens of Marion, who was chairman of the Industrial War Bonds Committee; Morris Abrams of the U.S. Treasury Department; and Howard Tooley of Indianapolis, director of special events for the war savings staff.

The comedians had to leave immediately for their next venue, so they were not even able to sell war bonds at the luncheon. Vincennes officials did wire them the next day at the French Lick Springs Hotel, where they were the featured act at a big war bond event staged by Tom Taggart. Abbott and Costello were informed that $37,175 in war bonds had been sold in Knox County the day of their appearance. They sold millions of dollars in war bonds during two big tours during World War II.

Lou Costello died in 1959 and Bud Abbott in 1974. Their legacy on celluloid lives on.

64
VINCENNES CCC CAMP LASTED JUST A FEW MONTHS

On June 11, 1942, the Civilian Conservation Corps (CCC) camp on North Sixth Street in Vincennes closed after only a little more than six months in operation. The short-lived project was started prior to American entry into the Second World War. It was the war that made the CCC obsolete.

The CCC was formed in 1933, part of President Franklin Roosevelt's New Deal legislation aimed at providing employment during the Great Depression. Passed during Roosevelt's first one hundred days, its purpose was to give natural resource conservation work to unemployed, unmarried men between the ages of eighteen and twenty-five. Men in the CCC planted trees (some three billion total), combated soil erosion, worked on drainage projects, fought forest fires, built flood barriers and undertook many other tasks aimed at preserving the environment.

It was in April 1941 that a CCC camp in Vincennes became a certainty. It was announced that Vincennes would have one of twenty-seven CCC camps in Indiana that year that would serve some 5,400 men statewide. The principal reason Vincennes was selected was because Knox County had been designated a soil conservation district.

Communities were responsible for providing the site for the camps. The Vincennes Chamber of Commerce took an option on a lease for eight acres belonging to Ellis Kelso north of Kelso Creek on North Sixth Street across from the Indiana State Highway Garage. Army engineers and a soil conservation expert came to Vincennes in April to look at prospective sites, eventually approving that piece of property.

On June 25, J. Ray Monaghan, who was construction superintendent for CCC camps in Indiana and Kentucky, arrived in the city to begin planning the camp's layout. Three days later, local contractor T. Frank Willis was awarded the construction contract. Workers began by putting in the foundations and laying sewer lines. The buildings themselves were prefabricated and would be shipped in. Willis and his crew simply put them together.

The project was plagued by setbacks from the start. There were long delays in receiving materials and the camp would not be completed and ready for occupancy until five months later. On November 24, the men arrived to take up residence. Some of them had stayed at the Washington, Indiana CCC camp while the Vincennes camp was under construction.

The camp comprised twenty-two buildings, among them five barracks, four garages, officers' quarters, a mess hall and an infirmary. At its peak, there were as many as 160 men housed there; their focus was soil conservation work.

On December 7, 1941, less than two weeks after the Vincennes camp opened, the Japanese bombed Pearl Harbor, Hawaii, bringing the United States into the Second World War. As men either entered the service or took jobs in wartime factories, many New Deal programs were no longer needed and fell to the wayside.

As noted, the Vincennes camp closed on June 11, 1942. By that time, there were only forty-one men still occupying the camp and there were just two other CCC camps remaining in Indiana. Some of the men were transferred to the camp at Fort Benjamin Harrison, northeast of downtown Indianapolis. The entire program was on the verge of ending, as Congress stopped its funding.

A *Vincennes Sun-Commercial* editorial praised the closing, since, although the CCC had been extremely popular in its day, by 1942 the camp was seen as a waste of taxpayers' money.

As for the then vacant camp, it played a role in the war effort. It was occupied for a brief time by air force staff prior to the opening of the pilot training school George Field in Lawrence County, Illinois. The buildings were later moved to George Field.

Overall, the CCC served its purpose. In fact, it was one of the most successful of the New Deal programs, employing a total of three million men between 1933 and 1942.

65
Castor Beans Were Grown in Knox County during the Second World War

During World War II, the American farmer did his part to help win the war, producing the food that sustained both the Allied armies and the civilian populations of Allied nations, all the while dealing with labor shortages on the farm. Some crops were designated essential to the war effort. One plant that was elevated in importance by the war was the castor bean.

Castor beans, which are not true legumes at all, became vital to the military after the supply of tung oil and castor oil was cut off from the Far East. Although many people associate castor oil with medicine, the oil from castor beans has many industrial uses, including in lubricants and paint. Some oil was still getting through from Brazil, but there was no certainty that would continue.

In the spring of 1942, the U.S. Department of Agriculture asked Indiana farmers to plant 300 acres of castor beans to be used as seed for the following season. Castor beans weren't even grown in Knox County at the time, but the county was assigned 150 acres of that amount, in what was called a "guinea pig" project. The other two Indiana counties taking part were Sullivan and Gibson Counties, making up the 300-acre quota.

J. Raymond Coan, chairman of the Knox County Agricultural Adjustment Administration, oversaw the project. Coan requested that farmers who participated devote two acres or less to castor beans. Smaller acreage was better, since it was such a labor-intensive crop. Harvest could be challenging, with the plants reaching a height of ten to twelve feet.

The first Knox County man to contract for a half acre was Francis M. VanNatter, who lived south of Bruceville, with many more to follow. Eventually, around 150 farmers in Knox County contracted to grow castor beans. They got their seed from the Commodity Credit Corporation, which also bought their crop.

On April 29, farmers were invited to a meeting at the office of Knox County agricultural agent Henry S. Benson to learn more about growing castor beans. Agronomists from Purdue University and the University of Illinois were on hand to answer questions.

On September 22, meetings were held at several farms across the county, with experts on site to explain how to harvest the beans. These included the farms of Ralph Curry, Ed Wallace, Elmer Adams and William Miller.

Harvest results would be mixed that year for several reasons. First, it was a wet spring, so planting was late. Then, there was an early frost, which further limited the growing season. Lastly, some of the soil where the beans were planted was too poor for a good crop, so overall yields were below normal. The average yield in Knox County was seven hundred pounds per acre.

Farmers still made money, though. They were paid four cents a pound for beans that were not hulled, or eighty dollars a ton.

The goal set for Knox County in 1943 was 450 acres, but by early April, only 200 acres had been contracted. That year, the government was paying six cents a pound for the beans. Another agricultural expert was in various parts of the county that year to offer instructions on growing the crop.

In 1943, as in the previous year, the purpose of growing castor beans was to establish a supply of seed in the event that it became imperative to increase the acreage and grow them commercially.

The plants would never be grown on a large scale locally. During the Korean War, castor beans were again produced in the United States, mainly in Texas and the southwestern states. They were grown in Texas for a number of years.

Today, some gardeners plant castor beans for their ornamental features: both their height and the attractiveness of their giant, palmate burgundy leaves. One disadvantage in growing them is that the seeds are extremely toxic.

66
COOGAN STATIONED AT GEORGE FIELD IN 1944-45

A former child star of the silent film era and one of the biggest names in Hollywood in the 1920s became a footnote in local history during the Second World War. In the summer of 1944, twenty-nine-year-old Jackie Coogan was assigned to George Field, the Army Air Force Training Command Pilot School in Lawrence County, Illinois. George Field was activated in August 1942.

Coogan was America's first child star. Born John Leslie Coogan in Los Angeles in 1914, he started out in vaudeville. His big break came in 1921, when he was six years old and Charlie Chaplin cast him in his film *The Kid*. (He had a small part in an earlier Chaplin movie.) That was the beginning of a series of hit movies throughout the 1920s and early 1930s. Coogan earned huge sums of money: $22,000 a week and 60 percent of his film's profits in 1923-24 alone.

Much of the enormous fortune he accumulated was squandered by his mother and stepfather, leading the California State Legislature, in 1939, to pass the Child Actor's Bill, what became known informally as the "Coogan Act," protecting child actors and their earnings.

Coogan married four times. His first short-lived marriage came in 1937 to starlet Betty Grable. Jackie Coogan joined the army on March 4, 1941. Following the Japanese attack on Pearl Harbor on December 7, he transferred to the U.S. Army Air Force as a glider pilot. He later became part of the First Air Commando Group, which was deployed to India in late 1943. The following year, piloting Waco CG-4A gliders, the group

1940–1950

Jackie Coogan, 1924. Coogan, who had been a major child star, was stationed at George Field for a time during the Second World War. *Library of Congress, Prints and Photographs Division, Washington, D.C.*

airlifted British troops behind Japanese enemy lines in Burma. Coogan had the distinction of being the first pilot to make the treacherous journey. He was awarded the Air Medal for his service. Coogan, a second lieutenant, returned home in May 1944. He reported to George Field on the morning of Thursday, August 31, but immediately departed for Indianapolis to do a radio program.

Coogan's role while at George Field was a combination of glider instructor and lecturer. He traveled all over the country giving lectures, doing radio broadcasts and selling war bonds.

Coogan became a familiar face in Vincennes and spoke before several groups about his wartime experiences. On February 13, 1945, the Knox County Boy Scout Council held its inaugural father-son banquet at the Fortnightly Clubhouse at 421 North Sixth Street. More than three hundred people crowded into the building for the event and to hear guest speaker Coogan talk about his landing of troops in Burma.

A week later, Coogan spoke again at the Fortnightly, this time as part of a program before the annual banquet of the Southwestern Indiana Implement Dealers' Association, covering much the same topic. He used a map of Burma and southern China to help illustrate his talk.

On March 1, Coogan was among those participating in the Knox County Chapter of the American Red Cross Fund Drive kick-off dinner at the Vincennes YMCA.

Coogan could often be seen patronizing the Rendezvous Lounge, a cocktail lounge located in the Grand Hotel. He departed from George Field for good at the end of July 1945 and was discharged from the service in December of that year.

After the war, Coogan resumed his acting career, mostly as a character actor on television shows. Among the numerous television series in which he guest-starred were *The Red Skelton Show*, *The Andy Griffith Show*, *Perry Mason* and *The Brady Bunch*. Many people will perhaps remember him best for his role as Uncle Fester in the television series *The Addams Family*, which ran on ABC from 1964 to 1966.

Coogan died of heart failure at the age of sixty-nine in Santa Monica, California, on March 1, 1984. He was interred in Holy Cross Cemetery in Culver City. The epitaph inscribed on his monument reads, "Humanitarian-Patriot-Entertainer."

67
Father Flanagan Brought His Message to Vincennes

The Irish Catholic priest Father Edward J. Flanagan, one of the best-known religious figures of his day, spoke in Vincennes twice in 1947, in February and again in December.

Father Flanagan was the founder of Boys Town in Nebraska, the home for orphaned and wayward boys. The first home was started in Omaha in 1917, later moving to a larger house. In 1921, Boys Town was moved to land several miles west of the city, where it remains, fulfilling its original mission today.

Father Flanagan gained increased notoriety in 1938, when the movie *Boys Town*, starring Spencer Tracy and Mickey Rooney, was released. Tracy won an Oscar for his portrayal of the priest. Both actors reprised their roles in the less successful 1941 sequel *Men of Boys Town*.

Father Flanagan's first appearance in the city that year was on Tuesday, February 11, when he was the opening speaker for the TeDeum men's society's spring public forum series. The program was held at the George Rogers Clark School auditorium at 8:15 p.m. Hundreds of people attended, many from out of the city, in what was said to be the biggest turnout ever for a public forum. The then sixty-year-old priest was introduced by Knox County Circuit Court judge Ralph Seal.

The title of Father Flanagan's speech was "Seeds of Juvenile Crime." He discussed the importance of a proper home life for the child, coupled with "spiritual training" to avoid juvenile delinquency.

Father Flanagan spoke again at Vincennes for a TeDeum forum that year at the same venue on Tuesday, December 9. A reception was also held for him at the Grand Hotel.

At his evening presentation, Father Flanagan drew a crowd of seven hundred. Monsignor Paul Deery, of the Old Cathedral, introduced him, and the audience sang "Happy Birthday," acknowledging the thirtieth anniversary of the establishment of Boys Town.

Father Flanagan talked about what was happening at Boys Town before launching into his principal presentation, called "Japan Today." Following World War II, Father Flanagan traveled to war-torn countries to give advice regarding the care of the countless children orphaned by the war. He had just come back from a trip to Japan and talked about postwar life there. He emphasized how children in Japan were taught to respect their elders and juvenile delinquency was not seen in that nation.

Father Edward J. Flanagan in Washington, D.C., with Assistant U.S. Attorney General Joseph Keenan in October 1938. *Library of Congress, Prints and Photographs Division, Washington D.C.*

The following day, he spoke to the Exchange Club at its noon meeting in the Rose Room of the Parkway Grill on North Sixth Street, with his remarks again about Boys Town. In his talk there, he praised the local St. Vincents Orphanage, stating, "It is one of the finest examples of what a homeless child's home should be in the United States."

He went on to the Eagles Home on South Fourth Street that afternoon, where he spoke with members.

Father Flanagan died of a heart attack the following year during one of his postwar sojourns. His death occurred while on a visit to Berlin on May 15, 1948. He was buried at Boys Town.

Later that same year, on November 12, the Boys Town Choir gave two concerts at the Vincennes Coliseum. A concert in the afternoon was for schoolchildren, and the evening appearance was open to the public. Both concerts were under the auspices of the Eagles, who received any profits.

PART VI
1950–1960s

68

VINCENNES CITY HALL RAZED

The face of Main Street in Vincennes was dramatically altered in June 1950 when the old city hall building, which had stood at the corner of Fourth and Main Streets, housing city offices for nearly sixty-five years, was razed.

The imposing three-story city hall, its most distinguishing feature being its clock tower and cupola, was built in 1886–87 at a cost of just under $50,000. At that time, it was considered one of the most outstanding city buildings in the state. The commodious structure served the community in a variety of capacities. In 1889, the Vincennes Public Library was established there in rooms on the second floor, where it would remain until the library's Carnegie building was constructed at Seventh and Seminary Streets in 1917–18.

Several decades into the twentieth century, the structure, once the pride of Vincennes, had become a burden to the city. Not only had the cost of maintenance and utilities for such a large building become excessive, but the city no longer needed all the space it offered as well. Further, it was the opinion of many that such a valuable piece of Main Street real estate was better suited to the retail sector.

There was talk through the years of the need for a building that was more modern, and as early as 1940, city officials were initiating plans to tear down the structure. The lot at the rear of city hall, at Fourth and Busseron Streets, also owned by the city, was green space, and the proposed plan was to use that as the site for a new building on Busseron Street. The Fourth and Main Street lot would be sold to help fund construction.

The Vincennes City Hall stood at Fourth and Main Streets. This photograph was taken in June 1938. *Library of Congress, Prints and Photographs Division, Washington D.C.*

Plans for a new building were even drawn up, and in July 1941, it was announced that a federal Work Projects Administration grant in the amount of $71,712 had been received to aid in the project.

As a result of U.S. entry into the Second World War in December 1941, none of the grand plans conceived regarding a new city hall was realized and nothing was done for the duration of the war. In the immediate postwar years, discussion of the need to take some action on the matter was again revived, but little was accomplished and the old landmark had a reprieve of a few more years.

Finally, in 1950, under the administration of Mayor William Betz, city hall was relocated to South Fourth Street just off Main, between police and fire department headquarters. Work on that building was being completed at the end of May.

General contractors Montgomery & Doyle received the contract to raze the old building. Some of the windows were taken out on June 5, and the real work of tearing it down began the next day. A crowd gathered at the corner of Fourth and Busseron Streets to watch as the walls were smashed down.

The Main Street part of the lot was bought by New York real estate developer Jack D. Weiler for $50,000 (more than the cost of the old city hall when it was built) and the Busseron Street lot by Henry Ostendorf, who paid $17,500 for the property. In August 1950, the Snyder Construction Company was awarded contracts for new buildings to front Main Street at Fourth. It was announced that the first stores to open there would be the Diana Shop and the Cotton Shop, both selling women's clothing, and Schiff's Shoes.

As for city hall, it remained on South Fourth Street (remodeled in 1973) until the present city hall was built on Vigo Street.

69
LOCAL LANDMARK CAME CRASHING DOWN IN 1952

On Thursday, March 6, 1952, approximately three hundred people assembled on the site of the old Vincennes Water Works to watch a city landmark come down. It was not a building that was vanishing from the scene that day but rather the 210-foot-high water works standpipe.

The Vincennes Water Works was constructed near the Harrison Mansion in 1885–86. A brief piece in the September 24, 1885 edition of the *Vincennes Commercial* noted that ground for the standpipe and pump houses had just been broken.

When the utility was built, the city could boast of one of the tallest standpipes in the United States. It is clearly visible in old photos of the Harrison Mansion, a then modern structure, towering over the historic house. Along with its great height, the standpipe had a twenty-two-foot diameter and a capacity of 600,000 gallons.

Time, naturally, took its toll on the standpipe. Over the years, it had begun to leak at the points where the iron plates connected, and much expense had gone into repairs.

The fate of the old standpipe was sealed in 1950, when the water department initiated extensive upgrades and modernization of its facilities. When the water works was established, water for the city was pumped from the Wabash River, filtered, treated and then pumped into the standpipe. Under the new system, water would be pumped from wells south of the city, replacing the less sanitary river water. The new million-gallon water tower was constructed in 1951.

1950–1960s

The Vincennes Water Works standpipe was erected in 1885–86 and stood 210 feet tall, towering over the nearby William Henry Harrison Mansion. *Knox County Public Library's McGrady-Brockman House.*

The water works land and buildings were eventually leased by Vincennes University, which moved the campus to Harrison Park in 1953. The lease agreement was made because the city had water works revenue bonds. The bonds had to be retired before the university took title to the property.

The principal water works building later became Green Auditorium (now Robert E. Green Activities Center). The building that would be named Florence Hall, in honor of VU Board member Florence Watts, was moved from George Field in 1952 to be used for home economics classes. At George Field, it had served as the WAC building. That structure is now the Francis Vigo DAR Chapterhouse and is located near where the old standpipe stood.

The process of razing the standpipe was a fairly simple one. First, a cable was attached to an elevated position on the pipe, which was connected to a winch. Then, a cutting torch was used to remove a wide strip near the base, about two-thirds of the circumference, and the standpipe, after towering over the city for more than six decades, was pulled down.

This is how the *Vincennes Sun-Commercial* described the fall: "It landed with a loud report—as if a 155 mm. howitzer had gone off. Air, suddenly compressed in the big pipe, whooshed out the end whipping leaves and grass away in its path."

The old standpipe was pulled down in 1952. This photo appeared on the front page of the *Vincennes Sun-Commercial's* March 7, 1952 edition. *Knox County Public Library's McGrady-Brockman House.*

Photographer William Offutt captured a dramatic picture of the standpipe as it was tipping over, an image that appeared on the front page of the next day's edition of the *Sun-Commercial.*

Longtime Vincennes Water Department superintendent Melvin Schwartz was on hand to watch it come down. Schwartz lived in the nearby superintendent's home and had thus resided in the shadow of the standpipe for years. It was like an old friend to him.

Approximately 153 tons of metal was salvaged from the standpipe, much of which was actually in pretty good shape. It was all bought by Dumes Inc. for scrap.

70

VINCENNES WELCOMED "CITIZEN" TRUMAN

On the morning of Wednesday, January 21, 1953, a train carrying sixty-eight-year-old Harry Truman made a brief stop at Union Depot in Vincennes. Just over four years earlier, on November 4, 1948, President Truman's train had also stopped in the city as he made a triumphant return to Washington, D.C., following a historic election victory over Republican challenger New York governor Thomas Dewey. This time, it was not President Truman who came to Vincennes, but "Citizen" Truman. After serving nearly eight years as president, Truman was out of power and on his way back home to Independence, Missouri. The previous day, he had attended the presidential inauguration of Dwight D. Eisenhower.

Truman was serving as vice-president in 1945 and elevated to the presidency in April of that year upon the death of Franklin Roosevelt. He faced a challenging second term, and his popularity waned as the United States became mired in the Korean War. He chose not to run again in 1952, and in that year's presidential election, the Republican Eisenhower defeated Democratic candidate Adlai Stevenson.

On November 4, 1948, an estimated ten thousand people had turned out to see Truman, and he made some remarks from the train's rear platform. In 1953, while no estimate of the number at the depot was given, the *Vincennes Sun-Commercial* called it a "large crowd" and went on to say: "It was conservatively estimated that there were about as many Republicans as Democrats in the gathering." Crowds were on hand at all of the whistle stops as Truman made his way west, and he was surprised by these turnouts and by the genuine affection people showed him.

Truman rode on the Baltimore and Ohio's National Limited. His car, the Ferdinand Magellan, on loan from Eisenhower, was at the back of the train. It was the same car he had used in 1948. At Vincennes, he walked through several cars and disembarked near the front of the train. Even though it was cold (the high temperature that day was forty-four degrees), he went without a coat and hat.

Unlike that earlier year, he did not make a public address but rather walked among the people, shook hands and chatted a bit. It was all informal, made more so by the fact that Truman no longer had either Secret Service protection or a large staff. He did have newspaper men with him, still reporting his every move and comment. They filed their copy at the local Western Union office.

The informality of the stop was illustrated by the fact that many who were present simply shouted, "Hi Harry!"—to which he responded with a smile and a wave. The county's Democratic leaders did greet him. One Vincennes person who got to exchange some pleasantries with the former president was local florist Paul Schultz. Schultz told Truman that he had a cousin who lived in Independence, and it turned out that Truman knew the cousin.

At some of his stops, Truman was naturally asked what he planned to do with his time. Earlier, in Washington, Indiana, when asked if he "was going to take it easy," he replied, "I don't know. It isn't hard work that gets a man in trouble. It's lack of it. When he doesn't have enough to do, he gets into devilment."

Truman was in Vincennes for just minutes before boarding the train once again, even helping a brakeman climb up. Bess Truman was on board, but she did not appear before the crowd.

Thousands of people turned out for Truman when he reached Independence on Wednesday night.

When he left office, Harry Truman was one of only two living ex-presidents, the other being Herbert Hoover. Truman kept busy writing his memoirs and establishing his presidential library. He was in good health. He died at the age of eighty-eight on December 26, 1972.

The 1955 Peach Crop Killed by Frigid Early Spring Weather

March 1955 roared into Knox County like the proverbial lion. There was wind, rain and hail, accompanied by a thirty-two-degree temperature drop. On the last day of February, the mercury fell from seventy-one to thirty-nine degrees, illustrating that winter was not yet willing to let go of its icy grip. Although March started out with cold temperatures, those would pale in comparison to the truly frigid conditions that were to come later in the month. That bitter cold was to destroy not only Knox County's peaches but also the peach crop throughout much of the country.

It was after midnight on March 1 that the severe weather came, causing property damage in Knox County. Strong winds wreaked havoc that day, with the area around Monroe City hit especially hard. Cyrus Noble, who resided near that town, had a large shed destroyed, and other buildings were damaged in and around the community.

Temperatures were up and down throughout the month, with five days total in which the temperature reached seventy degrees or higher. In contrast, the mercury dropped to fourteen degrees on March 7 and twenty-five degrees on March 17.

On March 25, just days after the official start of spring, two inches of snow fell in Knox County, making for Christmas-like scenery and creating hazardous driving conditions.

It was then the bitter cold of Saturday, March 26, that was catastrophic for orchardists. At 7:00 a.m., the temperature at Vincennes stood at eight degrees above zero, killing the buds that were forming on peach trees. The freezing temperatures continued throughout the day, with the mercury rising to only twenty-one degrees by afternoon. The headline of the Sunday, March 27, 1955 edition of the *Sun-Commercial* said it all: "SNOW, RECORD COLD THROTTLES SPRING." The paper colorfully reported: "Old Man Winter reached into his bag of tricks over the weekend to send Spring reeling for the count in a post-season rally."

The temperature fell to eleven degrees at Evansville. Peach trees at Henderson, Kentucky, had already been in full bloom.

Other parts of Indiana had it much worse as far as snowfall. In the north and central parts of the state, there were three-to-four-foot drifts and numerous traffic deaths. The eastern two-thirds of the country was hit by the wintry weather.

Part of the irony of that late March cold wave was that local orchardists had earlier breathed a sigh of relief when their peach trees came through mostly unscathed during bitter cold in mid-February. On February 10–11, Knox County experienced a fifty-five-degree temperature drop in a twenty-four-hour period, from fifty degrees to negative five. Contrary to early dire predictions following that cold snap, samples taken showed an abundance of live buds remaining on Knox County's peach trees.

Orchardists were not to be that lucky following the late March temperature drop. Knox County agricultural agent Martin J. Huxley later spoke to local growers who told him that, although they had discovered some live peach buds, there would not be a commercial peach crop in the county that year. The total loss for Knox County orchardists was estimated to be $1 million.

On the plus side, with the exception of early apples, the county's apple trees had come through unharmed. It was determined that the March cold weather had also led to a nearly total loss of peaches in ten southeastern states.

In July, the Dixie Orchard Company on Hart Street Road had a small amount of an early peach called Jerseyland. Locally, these sold for as much as twenty-five cents apiece. In August, Dixie offered a limited quantity of Hale peaches. Some other local orchardists also had small amounts of peaches for sale that summer.

There were California peaches available at Vincennes grocery stores in August. The A&P sold California Elberta peaches at two pounds for thirty-nine cents.

Also true to the old proverb, just days after the single-digit reading, the month of March 1955 went out like a lamb, with temperatures rebounding into the sixties.

72
"Uncle Billy" Green Jr.
Was Grandma Moses of Vincennes

Vincennes had two "Uncle Billy" Greens. The first was William Green Sr., one of the city's early residents who was heavily involved in local business and civic life. The second was his youngest son, William Jr., a lifelong resident of Vincennes who lived to the age of ninety-four. Both men were highly regarded and in their later years addressed by most everyone with the affectionate title "Uncle Billy."

William Sr. moved to Vincennes in 1831, and he and his wife, Hannah, raised a large family. William had a stage and livery operation, built Green's Opera House and was Vincennes's first fire chief and a city councilman.

William Green Jr. was born at the family's Seventh and Main Street home on March 8, 1861. As a young man, he transported mail between Union Depot and the post office. (His father had the contract for this work.) He held a variety of other jobs, including superintendent of the Vincennes Citizens' Street Railway Company. For many years, he was bookkeeper for the F. Samonial Coal Company. He never married.

One of William Green Jr.'s real talents emerged late in life. It was after the age of seventy, when he bought a ninety-eight-cent book on the subject from Sears, Roebuck and Company, that he took up oil painting. His style was much like the primitives of Grandma Moses, who was also in her seventies when she began painting, eventually to great acclaim.

Although Green's subject matter varied, one of his themes was life in old Vincennes. He painted on board or cardboard, whatever was available, instead of canvas. He didn't sell his paintings but, as the *Vincennes Sun-*

Above: William "Uncle Billy" Green Jr.'s painting *A Summer Evening in Old Vincennes*. *Knox County Public Library's McGrady-Brockman House.*

Opposite: William "Uncle Billy" Green Jr.'s painting *Leaving Home*. *Knox County Public Library's McGrady-Brockman House.*

Commercial noted, painted "for the sheer joy and self-expression, and to preserve some of his recollections of early Vincennes."

There was speculation that Green took his inspiration from one Bill Manning, whom he knew in his youth. Manning didn't have any training as an artist, either, and did his works in chalk, selling them for pocket change.

William Green Jr. died on May 26, 1955, and was buried in Greenlawn Cemetery alongside his parents. Longtime Vincennes University Board member Judge Curtis Shake, known for his interest in local history, is credited with the university's acquisition of many of Green's works. In January 1956, VU had a showing of twenty-five of Uncle Billy's paintings. Twenty years later, in 1976, there was an exhibit of Green's paintings at VU's Shircliff Art Gallery.

1950–1960s

Today, the Knox County Public Library has long-term loan of a number of his colorful works. The paintings, now beautifully framed, hang in the library's McGrady-Brockman House, where they can be enjoyed by the public.

73
Davy Crockett Craze Hit Locally

Between December 1954 and December 1955, Walt Disney Productions broadcast a five-part series on the television show *Walt Disney's Disneyland* featuring the famous frontiersman and later member of Congress Davy Crockett. Fess Parker stars in the title role, and Buddy Ebsen plays his sidekick, George "Georgie" Russell. In late May 1955, the first three episodes of the series were combined and released as a feature film.

What happened after the programs began airing was totally unexpected and nothing like anyone had ever seen before. The country was swept by a Davy Crockett Craze, with countless Crockett product tie-ins—most notably Davy's coonskin cap—being swept from store shelves by the parents of children who were captivated by the on-screen exploits of the frontier hero. The public simply could not get enough of Davy Crockett.

The craze hit Vincennes, just as it did every other community, in the spring and summer of 1955. Local stores, including Gimbel-Bond, Montgomery Ward, Hills and Kresge's, all on Main Street, had big displays of Davy Crockett merchandise quickly snapped up by shoppers.

In May, Gimbel's had a "Davy Crockett Trading Post" set up on its second floor and was giving free Davy Crockett balloons to children who visited. The store had all kinds of Crockett apparel, including a three-piece Alamo outfit (Crockett died at the Alamo in 1836) for $4.87. On June 11, Davy Crockett "as a boy" appeared at Gimbel's. On that day, the first seventy-five boys who came received a free Davy Crockett frontier tie, and the first seventy-five girls got a free Davy Crockett head scarf.

1950–1960s

Vincennes's Main Street stores, where shoppers could find their Davy Crockett merchandise. *Knox County Public Library's McGrady-Brockman House.*

On August 24, Wards placed a full-page ad in the *Vincennes Sun-Commercial* featuring only Crockett products. These included a lamp, Barlow knife, tent, guitar, knit shirt, belt, leather vest and beanie, school bag, lunch box and thermos and frontier shirt and pants. Davy's coonskin cap, with real fur trim and a snap on racoon tail, was on sale for $1.66. The regular price was $1.98. Boys all over the country could be seen sporting the cap. An estimated five thousand caps a day were being sold nationally.

"Kresge's Is Your Davy Crockett Headquarters" boasted that store. One of the items Kresge's carried was the 45-rpm record "The Ballad of Davy Crockett," the popular theme song of the programs, which was on the lips of fans all across the country. It could be purchased for a quarter. Kresge's also carried Davy Crockett cap pistols and rifles, sunglasses and sand pails, among many other Crockett products.

Even grocery stores capitalized on the sensation. The Piper Grocery Company, which had three Vincennes branches, sold ten ounces of peanut butter in a Davy Crockett glass tumbler for thirty-five cents.

The feature film *Davy Crockett, King of the Wild Frontier* played at the New Moon Theater at Sixth and Main Streets to packed houses from June 29 to

July 2. Adult admission for evening shows was seventy cents, and matinees were fifty cents. Children got in for thirty cents. The New Moon also had a promotion at the time giving children free admission on Saturdays if they brought in three Harvest Queen brand bread wrappers.

People could register at Hill's for a chance to win free tickets to the film. Hill's gave out fifteen tickets daily.

Along with the TV shows, the movie and merchandise were Davy Crockett–themed parties. On May 18, the Rivet Circle, Daughters of Isabella, had a Davy Crockett party, held at Lake Lawrence, for the 1955 graduating class of St. Rose Academy. All attendees were dressed in frontier garb, and miniature Davy Crockett statues were handed out as favors. In August of that year, Joseph and Edith Yount had a Davy Crockett birthday party for their eight-year-old daughter, Judy Jo, one of many such parties in the community.

In 1956, the last two Crockett TV shows were combined and released as a second theatrical film called *Davy Crockett and the River Pirates*. By that time, almost as quickly as it had begun—and after millions of dollars in merchandise had been sold—the Crockett fad had ended.

74
OLD STATE BANK BUILDING WAS ONCE TRULY HIDDEN HISTORY

For many years, the Old State Bank building in Vincennes, located on North Second Street, a block off Main Street, could truly be classified as "hidden history." Through much of the twentieth century, the building's façade, including the massive sandstone columns of the portico now an iconic part of the city's streetscape, was hidden by other structures. It is safe to say that some people didn't even know the building was there, although it could be seen from First Street and was then more fully exposed in 1959 when the neighboring Grand Opera House was razed.

As with the William Henry Harrison Mansion, it was thanks to the Francis Vigo chapter, Daughters of the American Revolution, that the historic structure was saved.

It was in 1834 that the Indiana legislature chartered the Second State Bank, locating one of its twelve branches in Vincennes, first in a rented building. The Greek Revival bank, fashioned of handmade brick, was built by John Moore in 1838 across from the equally impressive Ellis Mansion (now the home of the Harmony Society).

The bank building featured sandstone columns, a cupola supported by six fluted columns and a steel vault. That bank's charter expired in 1858, although the space would continue to be used as a bank until 1877.

There are many old traditions associated with the building, including the claim that the original roof was made of lead and was removed during the Civil War to be melted down for Union bullets.

The building eventually came under private ownership and, for a time in the late 1880s, was leased by the government for a post office. Being

A postcard view of the Old State Bank building following its restoration in the 1960s. *Knox County Public Library's McGrady-Brockman House.*

prime downtown retail space, two businesses, at 112 and 114 North Second Street, were later constructed over the bank's imposing front. For many years, a branch of the grocery chain Oakley's Economy Stores (later Oakley-Kroger) was located there, and the bank's original steel vault was used to store groceries.

The local chapter of the DAR purchased the building in 1958, borrowing $4,000 to do so, then worked to pay off the debt through donations and rental income from the two businesses on the site, at that time a used clothing store and a cigar store. Some of the DAR members who were the driving force behind the project were Loretha Hamke, Doris Wheeler, Florence Watts, Jo Ann Wright, Rose Schultheis and America Greenlee.

It had always been the intention of the DAR to save the building, but not necessarily undertake the costly renovations. In January 1964, the chapter gave the bank building to the State of Indiana, only later retiring the debt. The state began restoration work later that same year, with E.H. Montgomery Construction getting the contract. That summer, the storefronts were removed, revealing the original columns that remained. The renovations went rapidly, and in January 1965, the old cupola was taken down and a replica put in its place.

For many years, beginning in 1966, the Northwest Territory Art Guild made its home in the bank. Today, the beautifully restored Old State Bank is part of the Vincennes State Historic Sites.

Selected Bibliography

Census Records

Indiana. Knox County, 1850–1940 U.S. Population Schedules. Digital images. Ancestry.com.

Original Records Housed at the Knox County Public Library's McGrady-Brockman House

Knox County Circuit Court Records
Knox County Miscellaneous Records
Knox County Superior Court Records

Newspapers Held by the Knox County Public Library's McGrady-Brockman House

Bicknell Daily News
Bicknell Monitor
Valley Advance

Selected Bibliography

Vincennes Capital
Vincennes Commercial
Vincennes Daily Sun
Vincennes Post
Vincennes Sun-Commercial
Vincennes Western Sun

Books

Batman, Maxine, ed. *Knox County History*. Paducah, KY: Turner Publishing Company, 1988.

The Bicknell, Indiana Centennial Historical Book and Souvenir Program. n.p., 1969.

The Freelandville, Indiana Centennial Historical Book and Souvenir Program. n.p., 1966.

Garrigus, Ross H., and Rebecca Denham Ruppel. *The Journey of the Good Samaritan*. Vincennes, IN: Board of Governors of the Good Samaritan Hospital, 1971, 2008.

Greene, George E. *History of Old Vincennes and Knox County, Indiana*. Chicago: S.J. Clarke Publishing, 1911.

Hardacre, F.C. *Historical Atlas of Knox County, Ind*. Vincennes, IN: F.C. Hardacre, 1903.

A History of Bruceville, Indiana. Bruceville, IN: Rainbow Class Bruceville Christian Church, 1954.

History of Knox and Daviess Counties, Indiana. Chicago: Goodspeed Publishing, 1886.

Hodge, J.P. *Vincennes in Picture and Story: History of the Old Town, Appearance of the New*. n.p., 1902.

An Illustrated Historical Atlas of Knox County, Indiana. Philadelphia: D.J. Lake & Co., 1880.

Indiana, Knox County: A Complete Survey of Cemetery Records. Vincennes, 1973–.

Knox County Interim Report. Indianapolis: Historic Landmarks Foundation of Indiana, 1997.

Knox County World War I Veterans. Indianapolis: Indiana Adjutant General, 1927.

Polk's Vincennes City Directories. R.L. Polk & Company Publishers, various dates.

Vincennes Fortnightly Club. *Views of Vincennes*. Vincennes, IN: *Western Sun*, 1916.

The V.H.S. Reflector. Vincennes, IN: Lincoln High School Senior Class, 1916.

About the Author

Brian Spangle, a Knox County native, graduated from Indiana State University with a master's degree in history in 1985. He was employed at the Knox County Public Library for thirty years, retiring from his position as historical collection administrator in 2016. He presently volunteers at the library. Spangle has written a column on local twentieth-century history for the *Vincennes Sun-Commercial* since 1999. In 2015, he published his first collection of those columns in the book *Vincennes History You Don't Know*. He is a member and past president of the Vincennes Historical and Antiquarian Society and the Northwest Territory Genealogical Society. He currently serves on the Vincennes Board of Cemetery Regents.

In 2017, Spangle received the prestigious Hubert Hawkins History Award for distinguished service in local history from the Indiana Historical Society. In 2019, he was presented the National Historic Preservation Award from the Francis Vigo chapter of the Daughters of the American Revolution.

Visit us at
www.historypress.com

www.ingramcontent.com/pod-product-compliance
Lightning Source LLC
Chambersburg PA
CBHW040250170426
43191CB00018B/2364